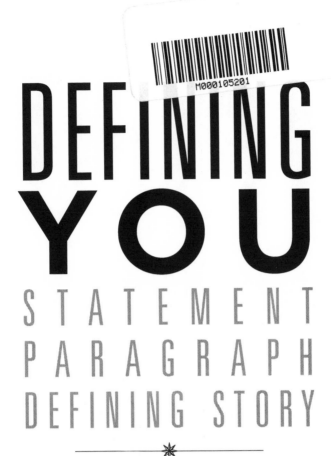
DEFINING YOU

STATEMENT
PARAGRAPH
DEFINING STORY

How Smart Professionals Craft the Answers to:

WHO ARE YOU?
WHAT DO YOU DO?
HOW CAN YOU HELP ME?

Mark LeBlanc · Kathy McAfee · Henry DeVries

INDIE BOOKS
INTERNATIONAL

ISBN-10: 1-947480-35-9
ISBN-13: 978-1-947480-35-3
Library of Congress Control Number: 2018912165

The Defining You Process™, Defining Statement™, Defining Paragraph™, and Defining Story™ are pending trademarks of Mark A. LeBlanc.

Designed by Joni McPherson, mcphersongraphics.com

INDIE BOOKS INTERNATIONAL, LLC
2424 VISTA WAY, SUITE 316
OCEANSIDE, CA 92054
www.indiebooksintl.com

Contents

PART I
DEFINING
STATEMENT

by Mark LeBlanc

Preface

Professionals fail for three reasons. You will not make it in your own business or professional practice if you have a lack of clarity, a lack of congruency, and/or a lack of consistency.

It will never be due to a lack of commitment. You are committed to making something great happen in your life and work. It will not be due to a lack of conviction. Over the last twenty-five years, I have met and worked with countless business owners and independent professionals. Every single one possessed a deep sense of conviction. It was a degree of conviction that he or she had a skill, talent, message, gift and expertise that could impact the life, work or career of another person.

Unfortunately, we didn't go to school to become entrepreneurs. While there is now a select group of colleges and universities offering classes in entrepreneurship, they are usually taught by instructors who have never succeeded in their own businesses or practices.

The way you communicate who you are and what you do will ultimately help you overcome *the greatest single obstacle in the marketplace*. Seriously. It's true. While you are faced with many obstacles, the inability to communicate effectively will result in a ripple effect of chaos and confusion you may never get a handle on.

While you are faced with many obstacles, the inability to communicate effectively will result in a ripple effect of chaos and confusion you may never get a handle on.

Oh, you can still make progress. You can continue to invest in copywriters, graphic designers, branding experts, and you can still make sales. However, it will always be challenging at best to attract prospects.

Imagine a prospect saying to you, "I'd love to get together with you and talk about what you don't know how to describe. Then when we get past that hurdle, I would like you to put together a proposal based on what you are unable to articulate."

While that may be overly dramatic, that scenario repeats itself day after day, for professional after professional who wonder why their prospects are confused and unable to make a buying decision.

It would also likely be a very good thing for others to refer prospects to you. But if you are unable to communicate effectively about your great products or your valuable service, how do you expect others to communicate your message on your behalf?

In your hands you hold a blueprint for positioning that may be second to none. We will provide you with what you need to know and what you need to do to set yourself apart from your competition, get the ear of your decision maker, and set the stage for your fees to be an investment in the outcomes you provide versus being considered a cost to solve a problem or satisfy a need.

It is not for the faint of heart. We will do some heavy lifting. You can do this. Let's get started!

Mark LeBlanc

CHAPTER 1

Why Define Yourself?

Let me count the ways. If meeting any or all of these outcomes, ideas and challenges is of interest to you then you are reading the right book. Please check the three reasons for defining yourself that resonate with you the most and rank them 1, 2, and 3 in order of importance.

_____ To put you at ease when introducing yourself

_____ To take the fear out of attending a networking event

_____ To anchor your message in creating your marketing tools

_____ To help you establish your expertise

_____ To set yourself apart from your competition

_____ To get the ear of your decision maker

_____ To establish value early in the mind of your economic buyer

_____ To position your fees as an investment versus a cost

_____ To make it easier for others to refer you

In late 1999, I wrote a little blue book titled *Growing Your Business!* It became an underground bestseller and led to hundreds of quantity book sales. Most volume sales were fifty copies or more while quite a number of orders were twenty-five copies or more. The book was an easy read and one you could digest in an hour or so. It was chock full of practical and easy-to-implement ideas.

Over the years, I have received many notes and emails regarding the simplicity of the book and the ideas contained in it. However, I believe the popularity of the book can be summed up in two words: chapter 2.

In chapter 2, titled Position Yourself for More Prospects, I shared a personal story of branding pain and a path for helping professionals answer the question, "What do you do?" It is a question that strikes fear into the hearts and minds of people in business around the world. For many it is so difficult to invest the time and energy to answer the question that they will invest thousands of dollars on everything but the ability to articulate the answer.

I shared thoughts on how you can answer the question by firmly stating your titles. If the first few sentences reveal your name and your title or titles, then your primary positioning strategy is positioning by titles. If you quickly move to listing your products or services, you often find yourself competing with other professionals who offer the same or similar products and services. In the majority of instances, you can find yourself defaulting to who has the better collateral materials or competing by proposal which in many cases leads to positioning by price or lower price.

My world changed forever the day I accidentally stumbled upon or was divinely guided to a new way to introduce myself at a networking meeting. I had attended this meeting nearly ten months in a row and every time I had the opportunity to say something, I tried on a new introduction. In fact, even with best intentions I found myself repelling prospects versus attracting prospects. It was incredibly painful.

As fate would have it, and before I was ready to throw in the towel on my dream of being a business speaker and coach, I answered the question with a different approach. I skipped my titles and my services. After I stated my name and without a lot of enthusiasm, I muttered the words, "I work with people who

My world changed forever the day I accidentally stumbled upon or was divinely guided to a new way to introduce myself at a networking meeting.

want to start a business and small business owners who want to grow their business." And I sat down.

People approached me after the meeting and wanted to find out more. I didn't understand how or why—but I was smart enough to try it again at another networking meeting. More people wanted to find out more. And within thirty days or so, I closed seven prospects on helping them start or grow their business.

This was a welcome change, or even a miracle, because for the first twelve months of my new business, I had not attracted a prospect in a way that he or she wanted to know more. Of course, that meant in twelve months I had no business. When I share that I had no business, I mean no business. None. Nada. Zip. Zero. Not a nickel.

Now I was in business and serving my first seven clients. It would take me a while to understand the depth of what had occurred, and why it mattered. Little did I know then what I know to be true today. I had gone beyond my titles and services to the articulation of the outcomes of my work. Starting a business and growing your business were three-word outcomes.

When you reach this level of positioning you have a greater likelihood of attracting more prospects, setting yourself apart from your competition and increasing the odds your fees will be considered an investment versus a cost.

It would mark the moment I developed or conceived the four phases of the marketing and selling process. For our purposes in this book, it will help you navigate the first phase I refer to as the attraction phase.

Understanding the four phases will create a framework for marketing and selling your products and services. Developing or crafting your *defining statement, defining paragraph,* and *defining story* will help you master the attraction phase of the process.

My colleague Kathy McAfee will share the framework on how to craft a defining paragraph and Henry DeVries, my business partner, will provide you with what you need to know and what you need to do in order to develop your defining story.

We will provide you with real examples of our own statements, paragraphs and stories, as well as real world examples of others who have heard, taken notes, done the work, and profited in many ways.

CHAPTER 2

The Four Phases of the Marketing and Selling Process

1. The Attraction Phase
2. The Meaningful Conversation Phase
3. The Decision Phase
4. The Agreement Phase

It is important that you have a framework for the four phases of the marketing and selling process. Let's take a brief introductory look at each phase before diving into how to create a *defining statement*. We will discuss the goal and trap for each phase. In time, you will know when you are in each phase, and will understand how to navigate each phase.

The Attraction Phase

Nearly everything you do from a marketing perspective serves the attraction phase. Developing a messaging platform, creating marketing tools and executing marketing strategies are built with one purpose in mind: to attract more prospects.

Your prospects may come into your world in three ways. Depending on your business model, prospects may walk into your place of business, call you, or send you an email. Of course, they may send that email to your regular business email, your Facebook Instant Messenger, your Twitter email or your LinkedIn messaging box.

The goal of the attraction phase is to get a prospect's ear, attention, or eye on your business. That's it. At that point the baton is passed to the meaningful conversation phase.

The trap is that it's possible to confuse, irritate, or repel your prospect. It can happen when you provide too much information too soon, when you prematurely ask for the sale, or when any message or action on your part is contrived. I could write on and on, although I believe you get the picture. Think back to your own experience of wanting more information and deciding to walk away or going to a website and exiting quickly. Those potential vendors, resources and partners failed at serving their attraction phase goal. While it would vary from service to service and product to product, it would not take long to take an example and estimate how much in revenue you may have invested if you had chosen to do business with any particular company in the short term. Now, imagine what you might have spent in the long term with a service or product provider.

The Meaningful Conversation Phase

The meaningful conversation phase is where your ability to sell makes a difference. For our purposes, we are using the word "conversation" literally. Yes, there are business models on and offline that are product driven and drive sales through meaningful copy. If you are making sales without a face-to-face or voice-to-voice conversation, take notice. Your meaningful copy phase will be made more effective in this phase as well.

The way you build a case for how you do what you do, why a prospect should buy from you, what you are all about, and what results a prospect can get from using your products or engaging in your services will ultimately determine how high or how consistent your sales numbers are.

The trap is that it's possible to confuse, irritate, or repel your prospect.

The Decision Phase

Within just a moment, a prospect will give you a thumbs up and buy from you or a thumbs down and walk away from buying from you. We are all guilty of making sales by accident. Imagine if you were able to pinpoint the moment and enroll more prospects by design and fewer by accident.

Many professionals shoulder themselves with the unnecessary fear of sounding like a salesperson. While volumes have been written on how to improve your selling skills or the old-school methodology of "always be closing," it is our belief that a yes or a no from a prospect is the result of building a case. When you have adequately built a case, you have every right and responsibility to ask for the sale. And you will never sound like a salesperson again.

The Agreement Phase

In this phase, it is your opportunity to discuss the scope of work, options, fees and financial terms. In addition, outlining the steps it will take to get started can enhance the overall buying experience. You have three goals in the agreement phase, including but not limited to:

1. Take the fear out of buying from you.
2. Take the surprise out of the invoice.
3. Make the first decision easy or easier.

If you can do one of the above, you will have good results. If you do two of the three, you will have great results. If you focus on doing all three, you will be unstoppable in the marketplace.

CHAPTER 3
Create Your Defining Statement
Seven Rules, Four Tips, and Three Tests

Creating a great defining statement can be challenging. If you take some time to review the rules, tips, and tests, the process will be made easier. For many the difficulty comes in wanting a final statement that says everything and will attract anyone anytime anywhere.

A little-known trap we can fall into is the perfection trap. You might want to dot every i and cross every t before you venture out into the marketplace. I hear it all the time, and I understand what you might be feeling. You want the perfect website, the perfect brochure, the perfect set of collateral materials, or the perfect way to introduce yourself.

If you fall into one of these traps, remember what I call a chiropractic adjustment for your head or heart: Done is better than perfect.

This isn't letting you off the hook in terms of doing your work. It should guide you in getting yourself out there or tying a ribbon around a tool before it is built to perfection. In fact, it may never be perfect, and that is okay.

Caution: You do not have to meet all seven rules, four tips and three tests. I like to live in a world of two or more right answers. Let's get you to a good-to-very-good defining statement. Then test and tinker with it. In time and with usage, you will come to own it.

Done is better than perfect.

The Seven Rules

1. Use eighth-grade language.
2. Use conversational language.
3. Use attraction-based language.
4. Use language that is dream-focused versus pain-driven.
5. Use language that contains what you do and who you do it for.
6. Use a dual-focus or two-part defining statement.
7. Use language that can be repeated.

Eighth-Grade Language

When you use language to impress another person, it will usually backfire and not make a good impression. If a prospect does not understand a word you are using, he or she may not have the interest or take the time to ask you to explain. Major newspapers are typically written at a sixth-grade reading level. When in doubt, a dictionary or a thesaurus can help you with alternate words to use and ways to simplify phrases.

Many computer systems have a built-in readability tool, similar to spell check or word count. The Gunning Fog index or Flesch-Kincaid readability tool will give you an accurate readability score. You can use this tool to score your defining statement, paragraph, and story. You can also use it when you write a blog post, newsletter issue, or article.

The Gunning Fog Index and Flesch-Kincaid tool are defined as readability tests designed to show how easy or difficult a text is to read. Both give the number of years of education that your reader hypothetically needs to understand the paragraph or text. The formulas imply that short sentences written in plain English achieve a better score than long sentences written in complicated language.

Conversational Language

If you will not say it, forget it. This is not the time to hire a copywriter to come up with compelling and creative copy for a physical marketing tool (although hiring a great editor may help you make it more conversational). Your defining statement is not a *wow* statement. It is a simple answer to a simple question. No one should be impressed by your defining statement, unless they are impressed by the fact that you have a simple, succinct answer that is clear and conversational. It will need no explanation.

The Language of Attraction

Your defining statement must attract people to you. If it doesn't, go back to the drawing board and keep working with it. Think about the problems, challenges, issues, and obstacles your perfect-fit prospects have and need to overcome. As you focus in on these day-to-day needs, then look to the sky and identify the 30,000-foot outcomes. Think of an outcome as a three-to-five-word phrase, e.g., start a business or grow your business.

Dream Focused

Similar to using the language of attraction, imagine the dreams of your prospect. Eight out of ten people who have a job have the dream to start their own business. The dream may be even a part-time or sideline business, but the dream is alive. While the number continually grows, and we may not even have an accurate count, if you own a part-time or full-time business, in most cases, when you put your head on your pillow at night your dream is to grow it.

You can take a pain approach and position yourself as a problem solver or needs satisfier. Though this approach works, it can lead to a prospect pitting you against your competition and driving a proposal process. Experience has shown me that prospects are more likely to invest in the outcomes you can provide versus paying to solve a problem or satisfy a need.

Position what prospects need in a way they want it. In time you will have more prospects than you know what to do with.

Example:

Problem: No business plan
Need: A business plan
Want: To start a business
To grow the business
Find money for the business
Accelerate his or her success

Now, use these examples to brainstorm and list the problems, needs and wants of your prospect. I could go to the marketplace and say, "I help business owners develop a business plan." At that moment, I am focusing on what a prospect needs versus what my prospect wants. In time, the *want* always wins!

What You Do and Who You Do It For

Your defining statement will serve you better if you *add who to what you do*. What you do will take the form of the outcomes you provide. By getting specific about who you are looking for and including them in your statement, it will direct your marketing efforts and help you create an aim in the marketplace. In the creation process, you may choose to use a generic or umbrella term to describe a group of prospects. As you progress or if you are clear about a specific target market, you can begin to slant your defining statement to that target market.

Examples of umbrella or generic terms* include:

• Business owners

• Entrepreneurs

• People

• Organizations

• Professionals

Note: We used a generic term in the developing of the subtitle for this book and wrote it in the form of an embedded compliment, i.e., smart professionals.

Position what prospects need in a way they want it.

Here are three examples of how I might slant my defining statement:

- I work with people who want to start a consulting business and with consultants who want to grow their practices.

- I work with people who want to open a restaurant and with owners who want to grow or expand the number of their restaurant locations.

- I work with people who want to enter the field of real estate and with realtors who want to grow their business.

Dual-Focus or Two-Part Defining Statement

Here you have a choice to make, and a rule to break. In my early days of teaching and sharing ideas on how to create a defining statement, my standard recommendation or rule number six was to make it a two-part or dual-focus defining statement. Over time and as thousands of smart professionals created a defining statement, some chose to break this rule. It was OK for them, and it would be for you. In fact, you have a number of formats to choose from, including:

WHO (Market)	**WHAT** (Outcome)
Single	Single
Single	Double
Single	Triple
Double	Single
Double	Double
Double	Triple
Triple	Single
Triple	Double
Triple	Triple (Not recommended)

It almost sounds like you are going through the drive-through at Wendy's. As I shared before, I live in a world of two or more right answers and here is where that is put to the test. Here are examples of each of the formats. Since you are going to see examples at the end of this module of other types of professionals, the easiest way for me to share these examples is through my lens.

Single Market–Single Outcome:
I work with people who want to start a business.

Single Market–Double Outcome:
I work with business owners who want to create extreme focus and grow their business.

Single Market–Triple Outcome:
I work with consultants who want to create extreme focus, accelerate their results, and grow their business.

Double Market–Single Outcome:
I work with real estate agents and financial advisors who want to grow their business.

Double Market–Double Outcome:
I work with people (generic) who want to start a business and small business owners (generic) who want to grow their business.

Double Market–Triple Outcome:
I work with business owners and entrepreneurs who want to create extreme focus, accelerate their results, and grow their business.

Triple Market–Single Outcome:
I work with chiropractors, dentists and veterinarians who want to grow their practices.

Triple Market–Double Outcome:
I work with consultants, coaches and advisors who want to reach their next level and grow their business.

Triple Market–Triple Outcome (not recommended):
I work with professionals, business owners and executives who want to create a new vision, develop extreme focus, and accelerate their results.

All these formats are used in the marketplace. Let me suggest to you that the more focused you are, the easier everything becomes. You tend to get what you focus on. What may seem like opening yourself to more opportunities can have the exact opposite result. Happy choosing!

Repeatability. Repeatability. Repeatability!

If your defining statement is conversational, you will use it and say it in the marketplace. If it is repeatable and others can repeat it or a part of it on your behalf, your number of referrals will increase. We often think our referrals come from our satisfied clients. Nothing could be further from the truth. You can get more referrals from connections, colleagues, friends, fans and followers—if your defining statement can be repeated. This is the rule to keep!

The Four Tips

Here are four tips for you to consider. Of course, these were the original four tips developed nearly twenty years ago. I have given you options and choices above that may conflict with these four tips. Use your intuition and the tips as lighthouse tips. Go with your gut and what resonates with you the most.

1. Use one "and" in your defining statement

2. Keep your outcomes three to five words

3. Use the words "work with" instead of help, teach, serve, provide

4. Use the word "want" instead of need

The Three Tests

1. Will I actually say it in a conversation or introduction?

2. Does it gain attention and attract a prospect?

3. Could another person repeat it or a part of it?

That's it. Now the heavy lifting begins and that is your responsibility. Even though I am providing you with target market examples, nothing beats the reward of doing the work. Here are several exercises you can work on.

1. Identify ten problems, needs, and results of your perfect fit prospect

2. Write fifty defining statements

3. When you have a good one, say it out loud 1,000 times or 100 times a day for ten days.

Examples of Defining Statements
Consultant
I work with business owners who want to accelerate their results and grow their business.

I work with leaders who want to develop stronger teams and get their people behind a common goal.

I work with entrepreneurs who want to find money for their next venture and scale their results.

Financial Advisor
I work with individuals and couples who want to improve their net worth.

I work with young people who want to start investing in the market and build a foundation for wealth.

I work with single parents who want to save for college expenses and build their own nest eggs.

Real Estate Agent
I work with people who want to buy their first home and sellers who want top dollar for their property.

I work with homeowners on how to maximize their property value and look for investment opportunities.

I work with people who want to create a real estate portfolio and find potential partners.

Coach (leadership, health or life)
I work with people who want to create balance and want more out of life.

I work with managers who want to become better leaders and have more impact.

I work with people at risk of burnout to create healthy boundaries and make better choices.

Where Are We Going Next?

The defining statement is just the beginning. What if you have a minute to tell a prospect about you? That is where the defining paragraph tool works best. A great defining paragraph is useful in many situations. This will be detailed by my colleague Kathy McAfee in the following part of the book.

PART II
DEFINING PARAGRAPH

by Kathy McAfee

Preface

If you had to make a choice between fitting in and standing out, which would you choose? Perhaps it depends upon the situation. Maybe you'd need to consider how much risk and how much reward is involved. Or who is in the room. Perhaps your reaction might be an automatic response based upon your past experiences, social conditioning, cultural norms, peer pressure, and other factors.

Like many professionals that I know, you may struggle from time to time with how to position yourself professionally; how to introduce yourself in networking situations; how to present yourself online via social media; and how to talk about your skills, experiences, products, services, expertise, and value proposition to others. You intuitively know that the impression you make with certain influential people could make a material difference in your future. How can you say the right words in the right way to make the connection and win the business (or land the job, get the promotion, or make a friend, etc.)?

This dilemma affects so many different types of professionals: from small business owners, entrepreneurs, consultants, coaches, authors, corporate professionals, attorneys, engineers, financial advisers, accountants, in-transition employees seeking new job opportunities, even college students who have yet to launch their careers. I believe that every working professional can benefit from doing the work contained in this book.

As an executive presentation coach, I've seen some professionals do very well in these challenging situations. They have clever elevator pitches or thirty-second commercials that get attention, make people laugh, and get the business. I've also seen other equally talented professionals struggle, sweat, and toil trying to explain what the heck they do for a living. They either become tongue-tied or they run on and on and on. It can be very stressful when it's your turn to introduce yourself in a business or social situation.

But it doesn't have to be this way. This part of the book will help you find a new path to positioning yourself for authentic, sustainable success. I believe that you can stand out and fit in at the same time by using the strategies and techniques that you'll find in this empowering book.

Working with my coauthors Mark LeBlanc and Henry DeVries has helped me understand at a very deep level how I want to be known professionally. It has helped me as a business owner, a professional woman, and as a human being become more self-aware and conscious of the choices that I have for the work that I seek and the clients that I engage.

My hope for you in reading this book and applying its simple but powerful principles is to have the same kind of profound transformation in your personal and professional life.

Here's to defining you, owning your voice, and claiming your personal leadership brand!

Kathy McAfee

CHAPTER 4
Develop Your Defining Paragraph

Rowena had dedicated her career to the field of higher education, helping students complete degrees that would lead to rewarding careers and meaningful work. She also had a particular passion supporting women in business and entrepreneurship. As a professor of management studies at a prestigious private university in Connecticut, she was well loved and admired by her students and faculty peers. She even cofounded a center for women and business in order to develop female leaders and help corporations leverage the full talent of their female workforce. Rowena was leaning in way before Facebook's COO Sheryl Sandberg did her famous TED talk and wrote the 2013 best-selling book, *Lean In: Women, Work and the Will to Lead.*

Unexpectedly Rowena received a phone call from a recruiter asking her if she'd be interested in a job at a different university some 500 miles away. It was a stretch job—skipping the position of Assistant Dean to becoming a full Dean of a business school for a prominent university in upstate New York. Rowena was excited, but nervous. She wondered how she could compete with other candidates who had far more experience than she had.

Rowena hired me as her executive coach to help prepare her for the various rounds of interviews that were part of the university's search process. She was very passionate about her work and had great energy. These were definite strengths for her. But she looked younger than her age and she worried that this could be a negative factor for the position she was going for. Her LinkedIn profile was, at best, ordinary. Her online profile gave the impression that she was perhaps not quite ready for such a big move ahead in her career. But the most intricate part was her difficulty in articulating who she was and what value she could bring to the new organization.

How did we solve this problem? We developed a defining paragraph for her—one that was powerful, concise, and above all, authentically Rowena. As she dove into the seven-sentence structure of the defining paragraph framework, she began to discover more about herself, her mission, her expertise, and the outcomes she had been able to produce for her clients (in this case, her students, peers, faculty, dean, provost, administrators, alumni, donors, and community).

Rowena realized that she was so much more than her title and current position. In many ways, Rowena discovered her personal leadership brand in the process of crafting her defining paragraph. With each out-loud practice of her defining paragraph, her confidence and conviction grew. Her voice, body language, energy and eye contact along with the compelling words and structure of the defining paragraph communicated that she was the ideal candidate for this job.

She made it through each round of the interview process, engaging and impressing the search committee, faculty, and student leaders who participated in the interviews.

In the end, she got the job. She had effectively leap-frogged over two steps to become the Dean of the School of Business and Economics of a major university in America. She achieved her goal!

Experiencing the power of the defining paragraph to position oneself and land the desired position, Rowena took my advice and modified her defining paragraph and showcased it on her LinkedIn profile. In chapter 6 you will see how Rowena modified her defining paragraph to work as the summary in her LinkedIn profile.

Rowena's success story is one of my all-time favorites. It reminds me of the power of the defining paragraph. Not only is it an effective tool to define who you are and what you have to offer, it helps you get meaningful work that fulfills your potential.

How can this happen for you, too? Let's start by examining the basic structure of the defining paragraph.

Follow This Seven-Sentence Framework to Craft Your Defining Paragraph

1. Your name

2. Your company's name

3. Defining statement for your primary profit center or area of expertise [P]

4. Defining statement for your secondary profit center or area of expertise [S]

5. A credibility statement

6. Your value statement

7. Your approachability statement

Take out your smartphone and take a picture of this seven-sentence framework. Why? Because I want you to commit this structure to memory. I want you to star it as a favorite on the browser of your computer brain. You are going to see it in your mind's eye. You will come to rely on it in a multitude of situations. Never again will you suffer or struggle when you are faced with one of these six situations:

Not only is the defining paragraph an effective tool to define who you are and what you have to offer, it helps you get meaningful work that fulfills your potential.

Six Immediate Applications

- When you have one minute to introduce yourself

- When someone asks you "What do you do for a living?" or "Tell me about yourself"

- When you want to be considered for a new high-profile assignment

- When you realize it's time to upgrade your LinkedIn profile. You can use your defining paragraph to improve your LinkedIn profile (or other social media sites) with a powerful headline (under your name) and a summary that helps you connect with influencers.

- When you need to convince someone why they should hire you and what makes you different

- When someone wants to know what types of referrals and business connections are best for you

Before we dive into crafting your defining paragraph, let's review a few fundamentals. Please keep in mind the following guidelines or "rules" as you embark on creating what will become the most powerful positioning tools you have ever had.

The Seven Rules

1. **Leverage it strategically.** The defining paragraph is for you first, and for your listener/reader second. Use it to become more self-aware and self-confident.

2. **Be introspective.** Spend ample time reflecting and being honest with yourself about your strengths and areas of greatest interests.

3. **Seek feedback.** Ask other trusted people what they think are your strengths, assets, and value add.

4. **Forget perfection.** Give yourself permission to draft an imperfect version of your defining paragraph. Test, modify, and evolve.

5. **Practice out loud.** Vocal awareness is critical. Audio record yourself, listen back, and self-critique.

6. **Experiment.** Play with it. Allow yourself to get comfortable with it. Listen, learn, and keep going.

7. **Commit it to memory.** See the seven-sentence framework in your mind's eye. Let it be your go-to guide whenever someone asks you "What do you do for a living?"

Let's Take a Closer Look

It's time now to examine the individual components of the defining paragraph. On the one hand, it is a very simple tool as it has only seven parts. On the other hand, it is complex and will require you to reflect deeply about your work. You may need to do some homework and interviews with people who know you well. But the reward that awaits you is well worth the effort. You just need to get started.

The defining paragraph starts off with the easy stuff. Sentences one and two should roll off your tongue pretty quickly.

1. **Your name.** First name and last name. Say it slowly and clearly. We want your name to stick in the mind of the listener. Imagine that there is a period punctuation mark between the two parts of your name. For example: "First name. Last name." When you see that period, pause for a split second. Breathe before continuing to the next part of your defining paragraph. Never rush it. Always take your time.

2. **Your company.** Rather than the phrase "I work for," consider more powerful action verbs such as "I run," "I serve," "I own," or "I lead."

   a. If you are in transition or are in between jobs, you can use the second sentence to state the industry, occupation that you have experience in. For example,

"My name is Joe Smith. I specialize in the commercial aviation industry."

b. If you operate your business virtually, you might want to list your web address in place of your company. For example, "My name is Joy Chow. I run my dog sitting business through a website called Rover.com."

c. If you are a college student, consider replacing the phrase, "I'm a student at…" with "I'm completing my degree in …." For example, "My name is Jane Hostoff. I am a future nurse practitioner."

d. If you prefer to position yourself by your personal brand, replace your company name with your brand handle. For example, "My name is Kim Kasparian. I am known as the Success Genie."

3. **The defining statement for your primary profit center [P]**

a. This is your opportunity to share a clear and specific sentence about your signature work or your best work. This is the work you seek more of. This should be an area of passion for you. When you share it verbally, you come alive with energy and enthusiasm. Even if you are tasked with doing something all day long, if you don't have passion for it, don't lead with it as your [P] sentence in your defining paragraph.

b. If you are a business owner, look at your profit and loss (P&L) statement for the last few quarters and most recent year. Understand what products and services (and customer sectors) make you the most money. Knowing your numbers will give you better insight into how you can craft your defining paragraph.

c. If you think of your business or profession like a cupcake, your primary profit center would be the cake in your cupcake. While it may not be as glamorous as the frosting or the sprinkles, the cake (or your primary profit center) is the part that holds everything together.

d. If you are reinventing yourself (your business or your career path), don't tell them what you've done or been in the past, rather tell them what you plan to do in the future.

4. **The defining statement for your secondary profit center [S]**

a. If you are business owner, look at your P&L statement for the last few quarters or years and identify which product/service area generates the second most profitable income stream for you.

b. Using the cupcake metaphor, your secondary profit center would be the frosting on the cupcake—the yummy sweet thing that sits on top of the cake, or your primary profit center. It is unlikely that you could survive in business by only offering the frosting, but it is what turns an ordinary cake into a cupcake. It's necessary and adds real, profitable value to your business model.

c. If you are an employee working for an organization, take a look at your list of responsibilities and projects and identify the second most important thing you do well. While it may not be the work you are best known for, this secondary skill area intrigues you, benefits you and you'd like to attract more of it.

d. You might also consider including some of your volunteer leadership roles or special projects you are working on outside of your normal job responsibilities. For example, you may serve on a board of directors for a community nonprofit organization whose mission aligns with your values and interests. Or perhaps you are serving as a committee member for your organization's employee resource group or diversity and inclusion initiative (e.g., women's network, young professionals' network, veterans' network, LGBTQ network, etc.) By including these volunteer roles in your defining paragraph, people may see you as a more well-rounded individual with capacity and capability for other leadership opportunities.

5. **Credibility statement**
   a. You only need one proof point or example to validate either your primary or secondary profit center or area of expertise.

   b. I recommend that you begin your statement with "In fact, …" or "For example, …"

   c. This is the place to use a specific, tangible, singular example. It can be helpful to incorporate a number or date in this section to make it more believable.

   d. Don't overcomplicate this part. You can showcase your credibility with a simple but confidently stated excerpt from your track record.

   e. Below are some examples *(Note: these are fictitious and are for illustrative purposes only)*:
      i. "In fact, I have a master's degree in instructional design and technology from _____ University."

      ii. "In fact, I have over ten years of experience designing and implementing e-learning courses for workforce development."

      iii. "For example, I've published a book on the topic of instructional design that is being used in classrooms at more than twenty universities."

      iv. "In fact, my work was recently featured in the *American Journal of Education and Information Technology.*"

      v. "In fact, I host a monthly podcast where I interview thought leaders in the field of instructional design and technology."

      vi. "In fact, I was awarded a gold medal in 2017 by *Training Magazine* for my gamification portal."

      vii. "For example, our customers have reported an increase of 25 percent in retention through my e-learning course, versus other programs they've used in the past."

  f. You can change your credibility statement from time to time. You can reference something that has recently happened, or that is coming up in the near future. For example,

      i. "In fact, last month I served on a panel of experts at the International Conference of Management Consultants."

      ii. "In fact, this summer I've been invited to serve on a panel with two other experts at the International Conference of Management Consultants."

6. **Value statement**

  a. Consider what is the *real* value of your work?

  b. List three or four outcomes or results that your clients or colleagues have experienced when they work with you.

  c. If you don't know, go and ask your clients (internal or external). They are in the best position to tell you what happens or what has happened when you work with them. Consider asking clients or colleagues this question: "What value did I create for you when we worked together?" Then stop talking. Don't interrupt, don't correct, don't minimize. Just listen. Often our clients are able to articulate our value impact better than we can.

d. It often works better if you reference more general outcomes than getting too specific. Save the specific data point for your credibility statement (sentence five in the defining paragraph).

e. Start with the phrase, "As a result of my work..."

f. Create a memorable pattern repeating the words "more" or "less" before our list of outcomes. For example:

    i. "As a result of my work, clients have more customers, more business, more profits, and more fun."

    ii. "As a result of my leadership, employees are more engaged, more motivated, more productive, and more collaborative."

    iii. "As a result of my work, clients experience less turnover, less downtime, fewer complaints, and less stress.

    iv. "As a result of my team's work, customers shop more often, spend more money, refer us more often, and give us higher ratings."

7. **Approachability statement**

a. This is where you get to share more of who you are personally, not just professionally.

b. Try to go deeper than the standard line, "I have three terrific teenagers and a wonderful husband." No one will believe you, anyway (at least not the terrific teenager part).

c. Have the courage to share something powerful like overcoming adversity or a health crisis. There is strength in exposing your vulnerability. It makes you more human, likeable, and real.

d. Keep it positive. Don't share any overtly negative, offensive, or shocking information about yourself in the defining paragraph.

e. Share only one personal interest, not a long list, as people will get confused.

f. You can talk about something that is going to happen or has recently happened in your personal life.

g. Feel free to update and change what you share in this seventh and final part of your defining paragraph.

h. Begin with the phrase, "On a personal note…"

CHAPTER 5

Sometimes You Need Outside Help

A few years ago, while attending one of Mark LeBlanc's fantastic business conferences called *Whatever it Takes*, I met Patti DiGangi. Patti has a unique expertise in dental coding and is a professional speaker, published author, and consultant to the dental industry. She's a fun person to hang out with at conferences because of her bubbly personality and great listening skills.

During this conference, Mark offered us the opportunity to video tape a practice presentation of our individual defining paragraphs. When it was Patti's turn, she absolutely fell apart. It was painful to watch. She struggled to find the words, and then she found too many words. She spoke too quickly, turned red, and couldn't seem to catch her breath. It was a disaster, and we all felt her angst. This was certainly not the competent expert that I had come to know and like during the conference. I approached her on a break to give her moral support. I also offered to work with her on her defining paragraph after the conference.

Over the course of a few coaching calls, Patti managed to gain control of her defining paragraph. Looking back at my notes, I found version one and compared it to version two. See if you can recognize the important changes that Patti made to her defining paragraph.

Examples

Version One drafted on Nov 9, 2016

My name is Patti DiGangi. My company is DentalCodeology. I work with dental professionals to understand and embrace opportunities through coding to increase practice profitability while improving the oral-systemic health of the patients we serve. Codes are the language of electronic health records which will be the most dramatic change in dental practice in the next five years. Interoperable records will connect dentistry to hospitals, pharmacies, medical practices and more. This is needed because dentistry is no longer just about fixing teeth; it is oral medicine. My training workshops and speaking programs help break the codes and demystify the process. Thousands of professionals have embraced these ideas through my successful series of *DentalCodeology* minibooks. Little bits of information because we know how busy doctors are, especially writing prescriptions. On a personal note, see this bag—it contains my "just-in-case medications." This feeds my mission to shape the future what it means to be healthy.

Version Two drafted on Dec 7, 2016

My name is Patti DiGangi.

My company is DentalCodeology.

I believe dentistry is no longer just about fixing teeth; dentistry *is* oral medicine.

[P] I work with dental professionals to demystify coding through my workshops, webinars, and keynote speeches.

[S] As an author, I also share my insights and expertise through a book series called *DentalCodeology*—little books of easily digestible stories about patients we see every day.

In fact, I just released my fifth book in this series called: *A Gingivitis Code Finally!*

As a result of my work, dental professionals are coding more accurately, increasing practice profitability, and improving the oral-systemic health of their patients.

On a personal note, my husband and I have explored forty-eight states in a motorhome. It took us seventeen years, and we are still trying to figure out how to drive to Hawaii and Alaska.

As You Evolve, So Must Your Defining Paragraph

Your defining paragraph is not set in stone. It is a living document. Unlike your resume, your defining paragraph is not focused on your past experience, but rather, your future. Therefore, it is important to keep your defining paragraph current. In preparation for the publication of this book, I checked in with Patti to see how she was doing and how her business was evolving. She told me that she created a new membership group that has become a major pathway to serving her valued clients. We both felt it was time to update her defining paragraph to reflect these important changes. Working over the telephone, we were able to quickly and simply update her defining paragraph to position her for the future. Notice how the core of the defining paragraph is still the same. We only tweaked parts of her primary statement [P], the credibility statement (In fact,…), and her approachability statement (On a personal note,…).

It's interesting to note that the discussion around updating the last sentence of her defining paragraph led to an empowering discussion about her interest in publishing her first work of fiction—a novel! As we wrapped our coaching call, I encouraged Patti to post her updated defining paragraph on her LinkedIn profile, so her network could hold her accountable to her goals and dreams.

*Unlike your resume, your defining paragraph
is not focused on your past experience,
but rather, your future.*

Example

Version Three updated on July 6, 2018

My name is Patti DiGangi.

My company is DentalCodeology.

I believe dentistry is no longer just about fixing teeth; dentistry *is* oral medicine.

[P] I work with dental professionals to demystify coding through my Dentalcodologist member group, workshops, webinars, and keynote speeches.

[S] As an author, I also share my insights and expertise through a book series called *DentalCodeology*—books of easily digestible stories about patients we see every day.

In fact, I just released my sixth and seventh books in this series called: *CDT 2018 Shifts Metrics Driven,* and *Teledentistry Pathway to Prosperity.*

As a result of my work, dental professionals are coding more accurately, increasing practice profitability, and improving the oral-systemic health of their patients.

On a personal note, my husband and I have chosen a new motorhome that includes a writer's desk so that I can travel while writing my first novel.

The Five Tips

As you experiment with crafting your defining paragraph, keep these five tips in mind:

1. Short, simple sentences work best. Split up compound sentences into a series of shorter sentences. Insert line breaks between the sentences so that visually you will be guided to see the seven distinct parts of this framework. Avoid acronyms and "corporate speak" to ensure others know what you are talking about.

2. Stay consistent with your primary profit center [P]. Allow yourself to modify or tailor your secondary profit center [S] depending on the audience.

3. Periodically refresh your credibility statement (In fact...) and your approachability statement (On a personal note...) to stay current with your experiences.

4. Pause between each sentence. When you see a period punctuation, stop and take a catch breath. Don't rush it. Take your time.

5. Make eye connection (one thought/one person) and smile when you share your defining paragraph verbally.

From Boring Biography to a Confident Introduction

I was appointed as an executive coach for a senior member at a law firm who specialized in government relationships. She attempted to explain to me what a lobbyist is and why the work that they do is important. I was confused and not sold on it (especially given what is often written in the news about the influence of lobbyists on politicians and lawmakers). So I went to her LinkedIn profile to try to get more information. There wasn't much there except for a nice photograph, a name, title and company name, and a basic listing of organizations where she had worked during her career.

Next stop was a visit to her firm's website where I found her professional biography and photograph. This time I found two very wordy paragraphs filled with her educational degrees, and a long list of awards, and the associations that she belonged to. It was visually unappealing and required too much effort to read. When I asked her about her online biography, she expressed her frustration with the people responsible for making updates to the firm's website. She also confessed that she wasn't paying much attention to LinkedIn and hadn't updated her profile in who knows how long. That's when I introduced her to the defining paragraph.

Over a few coaching sessions, she took control of her personal brand and developed a new, improved way of talking about her work. In fact, she came to better understand and appreciate the true nature of her role and the impact she has on clients and their organizations. We audio recorded her verbalizing her defining paragraph in the various situations she might find herself in (e.g., formal client meetings, informal social situations, business lunches, networking meetings, etc.). With each practice session she made refinements to content as well as her delivery and energy. I was observing a transformation in the making. From lobbyist to navigator and client champion. Plus, she has a great demeanor, is caring, and very likeable. Who wouldn't want to spend time with her?

Example

Below is an imperfect draft of her defining paragraph. Her name and firm's name have been changed to protect privacy.

My name is Janet Moore.

I run a government affairs group called Navigation Partners.

I named it that because many people tell me that they don't have a clue how state government works. That's why navigating state government is the primary focus of my work. I do this by helping my business, not-for-profit, and trade association clients gain access to decision makers at all levels of state government.

I also serve as a Strategic Planning Consultant, providing my clients with the guidance and resources they need to refine their goals, develop and implement action plans.

In fact, I was recently appointed to the board of directors for the State Law Resources organization which is a national network of law firms with government affairs practices.

When clients work with me, they become more familiar with the workings of state government, more confident in their ability to affect the process, and ultimately, they're able to realize their strategic goals.

On a personal note, I'm the mother of twins and I've just enrolled in a sign language course with my daughter which starts in a few weeks.

Tell me about you.

The Three Tests

1. Does it feel natural, authentic, and empowering to share in a conversation?

2. Does it help you and others understand your specific areas of expertise?

3. Does it open the conversation to deeper levels of discussion?

There's no better way to start the process than to just start. Remember we are going for an "imperfect draft" so you can cut yourself some slack. To make this easier for you, I'll remind you of the seven-sentence framework for the defining paragraph. I'm also going to give you a simple fill-in-the-blank beginning exercise in the next chapter. Start by filling out the easy sections first (e.g., sentences one and two—your name and your company—and sentence seven—your approachability statement). Proceed to the next chapter and give it a try.

CHAPTER 6

Now It's Your Turn

Remember that you are building an imperfect draft first. This is a work in progress. So whatever gobbledygook comes out on the page today, that's just fine. You can change it later. In fact, you will change it, and test it, and refine it many times before you are happy with it. That's just part of the process. Embrace it and start now. Just fill in the blanks—all of them.

Follow the seven-sentence framework:

1. Your name

2. Your company name

3. The defining statement for your primary profit center, area of responsibility or expertise [P]

4. The defining statement for your secondary profit center, area of responsibility or expertise [S]

5. Credibility statement (only one needed). Begin with, "In fact, I...."

6. Value statement: What is the real value of your work? List up to four outcomes or results.

   Begin with the phrase, "As a result of my work...."

7. Add a personal statement: Bring out more of who you are to create a personal connection.

   Begin with the phrase, "On a personal note...."

Fill in all the blanks:

1. My name is _____ .

2. I run/serve/am known as _____ .
   at/in _____
   ____(Company, organization, profession, industry).

3. _____
   is the primary focus of my work/areas of expertise/
   signature work/service/product I offer. (primary
   profit center or area of expertise).

4. As a _____ ,
   I also lead/support/run/excel at _____
   (secondary profit center or area of expertise).

5. In fact, I_____

   _____

   _____

   _____

   (list one example, social proof, accomplishment, or
   award that demonstrates your credibility).

6. As a result of my work, _____

   _____

   _____

   _____

   (list up to four outcomes from your work).

7. On a personal note, I _____

   _____

   _____

   (Share something about your personal life that could
   bring a smile and spark a conversation).

A Discovery Tool That Evolves as You Do

I have been working on my own defining paragraph for a number of years now. Because I am always evolving, I find my defining paragraph evolves as well. But it never deviates far from my core essence. It has become part of how I understand myself and my work. It is how I want to be known professionally. As I have become more confident when sharing my defining paragraph with others, I find that I am able to make stronger connections with people. I am much more discerning about what kind of clients and work are good for me and my business. I can say "no" more easily, and I can say "yes" more confidently. These are just a few of the intrinsic benefits of working with the defining paragraph.

Example

Here is the short version of my current defining paragraph:

My name is Kathy McAfee.

I am known as America's Marketing Motivator.

As an executive presentation coach, I work with corporate professionals who want to *stop global boring* by reducing their PowerPoint emissions and becoming more powerful presenters.

I also coach, train, and speak on the topic of effective networking which helps people get where they want to go by building more productive, professional relationships.

In fact, I wrote the book *Networking Ahead* which challenges us to rethink networking, not as an event or activity, but as a strategy for a successful life.

As a result of my work, business professionals are able to more confidently communicate their ideas, enhance their individual effectiveness, and enjoy more robust careers and businesses.

On a personal note, I'm an ovarian cancer survivor, and feel grateful to have a new lease on life.

Applying Your Defining Paragraph on Social Media Sites

When Mark LeBlanc invented the defining paragraph he did so with the idea that it would be a spoken tool, not a written tool. But we have both discovered the wide variety of applications that a defining paragraph has in the written form and online. In particular, it works very well on LinkedIn. In fact, once my clients are comfortable with their defining paragraphs I encourage them to modify their defining paragraphs and use them on their LinkedIn profiles as their personal summary statements.

Benefits of Using Your Defining Paragraph on LinkedIn

- Differentiates you from others who work in similar professional fields

- Positions you in the way that you want to be positioned in the market place

- Creates a more personal, likeable approach, making it more inviting for people to get to know you

- Increases the acceptance rates of the LinkedIn invitations that you send (especially if you add a personalized note with each invite you send)

- Allows people to research you, your background, and know what you stand for in advance of meeting you

- Provides a deeper and more interesting read, rather than a short list of bulleted skills (save that for your resume or CV)

Example

Here is an adapted version of my defining paragraph that I have used on LinkedIn as my profile summary.

Following a successful twenty-year career in consumer brand marketing and sales, I launched my own business in 2005 in the field of learning and development. For the past thirteen years I've been working with organizations to help elevate the talent and potential of their leaders, emerging leaders, and professional staff through training, coaching, speaking and blogging.

Today I am known as America's Marketing Motivator and I focus my time and energy sharing my two areas of expertise: communication and connection.

As an executive presentation coach and professional speaker, I help people present themselves and their ideas more effectively and confidently. I do this by teaching them the art of high-engagement presentations.

As a networking skills trainer and author, I help professionals adopt networking as a strategy for a successful career, business, and life. I teach them skills and best practices to build more productive, collaborative relationships that will create more opportunities for themselves and others.

In fact, I've authored two books, *Networking Ahead,* 3rd edition (2017) and *Stop Global Boring* (2016) and was recognized as Best Blog of the Year in 2014 by the Women's World Awards for my networking tips blog.

As a result of my work, clients tell me that they feel more confident, more motivated, more influential, and more connected at work and in life.

On a personal note, I recently relocated from Connecticut to South Carolina and am applying my networking principles to build a new community and local base of business, while continuing to expand my business globally.

Below are my contact details to make connecting easier.

Kathy McAfee, America's Marketing Motivator
Mobile +1 (860) 371-8801*
Email: Kathy@AmericasMarketingMotivator.com
or MarketingMotivator@yahoo.com

p.s. I invite you to subscribe to my blog at
https://www.americasmarketingmotivator.com/#signup

*Note: I deliberately included the +1 international prefix in my telephone number because I am actively building a global network.

Preparing for Big Opportunities

The process of crafting your defining paragraph will help you come into a greater understanding of who you are and the value you bring to the workplace through your skills, knowledge, abilities, and passion. It can also help to prepare you for big opportunities, such as major changes and moves in your career and business.

Below is an example of the defining paragraph belonging to Rowena, whose story was featured in chapter 4 of this book. With her permission I share her positioning statement that she developed to prepare herself for the interview process. The italics are my own, to help you clearly see the framework you have learned in this chapter.

Example

> My name is Rowena Ortiz-Walters and I *oversee* an academic department in the School of Business at Quinnipiac University in Connecticut.
>
> *As a leader in higher education,* I foster educational excellence by *compassionately engaging others* and reframing challenges to *make opportunities seem possible.*
>
> *As a researcher and a public speaker,* I also contribute to the national conversation on the status of women's careers through my scholarship and speaking engagements.
>
> In fact, I recently cofounded the *Center for Women and Business* to propel forward the full potential of the female workforce and female leadership.
>
> *As a result of my collaborative leadership,* the department is on a growth trajectory with 30 percent more students, our Human Resources Management program is nationally ranked number one, and career track offerings for students are in fields with solid job prospects.
>
> On a personal note, I am a first-generation college graduate and have experienced firsthand the power of education in changing the trajectory of your life.

As you know, Rowena was successful in landing her dream job as Dean of the School of Business and Economics at SUNY Plattsburgh in upstate New York. Following her appointment as Dean, she quickly updated her defining paragraph and adapted it to her LinkedIn profile as her summary. Notice how she showcases her bilingual skills and her newest credibility example while still being inviting and inclusive. Who wouldn't want to connect with Rowena after reading her LinkedIn profile?

(name with professional photo)

Rowena Ortiz-Walters

(headline)

Compassionate Higher Education Leader focused on Excellence and Results

(summary)

Welcome/Bienvenido to my LinkedIn Page and Profile. I am a Leader, Scholar, and Public Speaker in Higher Education.

I am the ninth Hispanic-American Dean of a United States business school. There is room for so many more Hispanic-American leaders in the field of higher education. Please join me!

In my role as Dean of SUNY Plattsburgh's School of Business and Economics, I support the achievement of educational excellence through my leadership approach, philosophy, and values, which include:

- Compassionately engaging others,

- Inclusive conversations,

- Investing in the leadership development of others, and

- Reframing challenges to make opportunities seem possible.

On a personal note, my mission is to support women's educational and economic empowerment. Toward this aim, I cofounded and served as codirector of the Center for Women & Business whose mission it is to develop female leaders, engage key decision makers in formulating policies that support women's careers, and help corporations leverage the full talent of their female workforce.

Through my scholarship as a researcher and speaking engagements, I contribute to the national conversation on the status of women's careers. Additional research expertise and interests include entrepreneurship, creativity, issues of diversity, and the scholarship of teaching and learning.

Sample outlets where my research appears:

- *Journal of Organizational Behavior*
- *Journal of Developmental Entrepreneurship*
- *Journal of Women's Entrepreneurship and Education*
- *Business Journal of Hispanic Research*
- *Journal of College Teaching and Learning*

Speaking engagements include:

- Catalyst®
- Permanent Commission on the Status of Women
- Institute on Teaching and Mentoring
- Chamber of Commerce
- Prominent Universities throughout Connecticut
- Academy of Management

If you have similar interests and passions, feel free to reach out and connect with me at (email address)

Don't Abbreviate Your Potential

Example

Let me provide a more typical example of a LinkedIn profile. This one is from a client of mine who is a very talented, motivated, and smart professional. She, like many corporate employees, has found herself in a job that doesn't really excite her. But it pays the bills and she likes the people on her team. She does the 9:00 a.m. to 5:00 p.m. thing (really more like 8:00 a.m. to 6:00 p.m.) and contributes what she can.

In her free time, she has found the energy to pursue an MBA through an online program. She is energized by what she is learning. She's beginning to dream bigger about what type of work she wants to do. She is in the process of reinventing herself.

Notice how she uses two abbreviations in her headline which might be a source of confusion. The reference to "Ex." could be an abbreviation for Executive or it could be interrupted as a former or past position. The abbreviation "Comp" could mean compensation, or it might reference something free/no cost? She'd be better off spelling out these words or reworking her headline to communicate something more compelling such as "Driving Organizational Performance and Employee Engagement through Effective Business Analytics, Compensation and Rewards." You be the judge.

This is what her LinkedIn profile read like *before* using the defining paragraph:

(headline)
> Ex. Director, Comp & Business Analytics - Driving Performance Through Rewards

(summary)
> Experienced compensation leader with a demonstrated track record of delivering exceptional service to

stakeholders to attract, engage and retain key talent. Skilled in Global Compensation, Management, Compliance, Executive Pay, Salary Structure Development, Market Pricing/Data Analysis, Collective Bargaining Agreement, and Mergers and Acquisitions.

And here is her new, improved defining paragraph. Notice how it positions her as an expert in her field.

My name is MiSook Chung and I'm a leader in the field of Human Resources and Operations. I believe that when companies take care of their people, the people take care of the company.

Serving as department leader of compensation and business analytics, I help companies make smarter investments in people and processes for sustained growth.

As an advocate for learning and development, I motivate people to invest in themselves through educational programs and stretch assignments.

In fact, I'm investing in myself as a full-time student at the Jack Welch Management Institute, where I'll earn my MBA in December 2018.

As a result of my leadership, companies grow, people thrive, and the magic of business happens daily.

On a personal note, I just launched an Airbnb house in Lake Tahoe and am having a blast hosting people from all over the world.

Win Points with Brevity

Example

I met a business leader at a global licensing summit in Cologne, Germany where I was speaking on the power of networking to build business. I gave him a copy of my book, *Networking Ahead*, 3rd edition. He in turn gave it to his sister who was in the process of reinventing herself professionally. She reached out to me on LinkedIn and we set up some time to speak on the phone. She explained to me using many words and examples of the work she had done in her professional career, and the work she wanted to be doing in the future. This was the perfect opportunity to capture a before-and-after example of the defining paragraph. With her permission, I'm happy to share with you the old way and the new way in which she positions herself for success. You decide which is more compelling, concise, and clear. (p.s. she's going with the new defining paragraph).

Before

In my experience, if you want to win buy-in that delivers tangible change, it's essential that you understand the perspectives of everyone involved. With this mindset, I've connected companies, talent and resources in the business solutions technology world for more than twenty-six years, selling millions of dollars of hardware and software, increasing revenues and impacting profits.

Working for a global analyst firm offering data insights, forecasting and solutions to the digital imaging industry, I've been able to use my passion for writing to share insights that help others.

My creative spirit and thinking out of the box mentality helped me architect the vision of bringing data to life with Vertical Marketing Segmentation services, a much needed solution in our industry today.

My colleagues recognize my expertise in solutions, sales, and managed print services showing my ability to evolve from an analog to digital transformation in the channel. My teamwork approach combined with enthusiasm and passion to make sure every experience is positive radiates in my business and personal life.

I value the opportunity to connect and collaborate. Contact me here or via Twitter @sgchangeagent.

After

My name is Sheryne Massa Glicksman and I am known as a change agent. Connecting and educating are my areas of passion which drive what I do professionally and personally.

As a software solutions expert, I consult with companies seeking digital transformation. I help them develop processes for connecting people, platforms, tools and ideas.

As a connector and educator, I write informational blogs using data analytics and inspiring personal experiences.

In fact, I've published articles in several industry trade magazines about technology trends to help sales reps be more successful.

As a result of my work, sales grow, connections deepen, work transforms, and people's lives improve.

On a personal note, I recently earned a trauma informed outreach certification, giving me the opportunity to bring yoga, mindfulness and meditation to youth in the foster community.

The Defining Paragraph Can Help Your Job Search

Example

I had the opportunity to introduce the defining paragraph to a highly experienced programme manager based in the United Kingdom. He knew for some months that his full-time position with a large global company was going to come to an end. So he opened up a LinkedIn profile to prepare himself for when he would go back on the market for work. A self-proclaimed "social media virgin," he knew he had to enter into this new channel but didn't know how to navigate it effectively.

For about a year, his LinkedIn profile drifted along. Only his name and title appeared, and the basic listing of positions he currently and previously held in his career. The absence of his photo made it more difficult for others to find him online. At that time there were two other professionals living and working in the United Kingdom with his same name: Richard Visick.

He needed to upgrade his LinkedIn profile so that he could leverage this powerful tool to help him in his new job search. He also knew that he needed to rebuild his network. So he did the smart thing. He turned to a few people in his current network and asked for help. I was honored that he reached out to me, and we agreed to engage in a series of coaching sessions via Skype, focusing on his networking strategies and personal branding.

After the first few sessions, Richard had a new understanding of his personal brand, what he did best, and what type of work environment and projects he enjoyed the most. Thanks to the defining paragraph he could now express this to others when networking, in job interviews, and online. And because the defining paragraph is a strategic tool, Richard was able to more clearly see his value in the marketplace and direct his job search accordingly. At the time of this writing, Richard's current working draft of his defining paragraph reads as follows:

Richard Visick

I am a Programme and Change Manager specialising in finance transformation; for the past fifteen years in Telecommunications and Retail.

As a Programme Manager, I lead cross-functional teams to deliver complex business and technology solutions.

As a Change Manager, I work with leadership teams and stakeholders to reinforce change.

Effective planning and good communications are how I ensure that the pace and governance of any project or programme is set, and that targets are met.

For example, I led the communications to 11,000 pension scheme members of a FTSE 100 client. The funding risk associated with the scheme needed to be addressed. The outcome was successful, and the campaign won the Professional Pensions Award for Communication.

As a result of my work, my clients are able to manage and measure performance, make change sustainable, and ensure that people know what change means to them.

On a personal note, I am passionate about sailing. As a member of the Royal Ocean Racing Club, I have completed four Fastnet and four Middlesea races.

You'll notice that Richard made some minor adjustments to the defining paragraph framework structure. He did this to fit his personality and his marketplace. He intends to use this positioning tool to help him be more effective in networking and job interviewing. And it's already working. Within the first thirty days of showcasing his defining paragraph on LinkedIn, Richard saw a three-fold increase in the number of people viewing his profile. Once he successfully lands a new job position, I am hopeful that he will continue to use the defining paragraph to effectively manage his career, his personal brand, and his digital presence.

Cross Cultural Applications of The Defining Paragraph

Example

I had the pleasure of being the keynote speaker at the Global Diversity and Inclusion Conference for Stanley Black & Decker headquartered in New Britain, Connecticut. My topic was "Networking Ahead for Your Career." I shared the defining paragraph framework with the audience to help position them for more effective networking and career advancement. Of the many talented and motivated leaders attending this conference, Maria Perdomo became a strong advocate for the defining paragraph and has been using it to develop herself and others professionally and personally.

At the beginning, Maria and I had a conversation about the style differences between Americans and Europeans, especially when it came to communication and self-promotion. For example, she felt that it would be inappropriate for her to write her LinkedIn summary in the first person voice as it might suggest arrogance and aggressiveness. She told me that most of her European colleagues take a humbler, more reserved approach to their online profiles and how they talk about themselves.

Having worked and lived in the United Kingdom for three years in my career, I understood and appreciated her point of view. Still, I wanted to push her a bit and get her to take greater ownership of her personal brand and career. I see too many professional women and others in the minority who work really hard and contribute mightily to organizations, but still get passed over for promotion and new opportunities. We know that unconscious bias and institution racism exists and works to keep certain people down while elevating others. There are also cultural and societal norms that mold some people into taking a more passive role in their own career development. I used to be one of them. But through experience, I've come to believe that there is also risk in waiting to be selected. Sometimes you have to select yourself and advocate on your own behalf. And that's just one of the reasons why I love working with the defining paragraph. It puts you in charge of how you want to be known professionally.

Maria and I had two amazing coaching sessions using Skype during the summer of 2018. She was working from France, and I was set up in my home office in Greenville, South Carolina. As she worked on her before and after versions of her defining paragraph (see below), she had a big idea. She felt that the defining paragraph could be used in the annual performance review and development discussion. She tested it out with her line manager and it worked like magic. It would be awesome if her company adopted the defining paragraph organization-wide, but until then, it's mano a mano, one defining paragraph at a time!

Please enjoy Maria's before and after example.

Before (as featured in her LinkedIn profile)

Maria Josefina Perdomo Arreaza

HR Project Manager EANZ | Diversity & Inclusion | Finance Manager EANZ

Actionable, energetic and results oriented business leader with a multi-cultural background, strong communication and interpersonal skills. Nineteen total years in a SKU intensive Industrial and Consumer products environments.

Passionate on inspiring and connecting people to drive company goals.

Areas of expertise: D&I, ERG's, FP&A, Commercial Finance, Restructuring & Recovery Plans, Merge & Acquisitions, Integrations, Process Simplification & Standardization, Sourcing Negotiations, Change Management and Global Strategy Development.

Broad experience in Project Management, Business Transformations, Harmonization of Cost Sharing, Standardization of the CoA and Best Practice Sharing. ERP Systems Consolidations and Mappings. Experience with Navision | SAP | BI | BW | Hyperion | HFM trainer | BA&R | QlickView.

Leading Diversity & Inclusion initiatives, Belgium Women's Network Chapter lead, Stanley Black & Decker Global point of contact with Greenlight for Girls, Stanley Black & Decker point of contact with PWI (Professional Women's International) and Jump (Promoting Gender Equality).

Languages skills: Spanish, English, Netherlands, French and Italian

After

Maria Josefina Perdomo Arreaza

HR Project Manager, Europe, Australia & New Zealand | Diversity & Inclusion Champion | Economist

As a Human Resources leader with nineteen years of finance experience, I am passionate about inspiring and connecting people to drive overall company goals while increasing employee engagement and well-being.

As a champion of Diversity and Inclusion, I bring my action-oriented, and best practice focus to lead D&I initiates and drive results across the globe.

In fact, we recently signed a global partnership agreement between Stanley Black and Decker and Greenlight for Girls to empower the makers of the future.

Because of this work and focus, we are living our values, growing the business, and building a sustainable workplace for all.

On a personal note, I speak five languages, have a passion for meeting people, love to travel and write, and have recently published several articles for the Dining Traveler blog.

Don't Define Yourself by Your Title or Your Degree

Example

Many professional people lead with their job titles. They confuse who they are with what it says on their business card. For example, if you are an entrepreneur you might be tempted to assign yourself a lofty title like CEO or President so that potential clients take you more seriously. Or perhaps you worked hard to earn an MBA or a Ph.D. and you are eager to show that off, and to differentiate yourself from those less accomplished. But titles and degrees do not truly reflect who you are as a professional, what you stand for, and what you want. They are just labels. They are not enough to serve as your positioning statement. You need to dig deeper.

I was reminded of this important insight when I was searching for a guest speaker with expertise in the topic of civil discourse who would be interested in being part of my Rotary club's Peace and Conflict Resolution Conference in Greenville, South Carolina. After watching the TED talk "Free Yourself from Your Filter Bubbles" with Joan Blades and John Gable, I reached out to both speakers on LinkedIn. I had a great conversation with Joan. Separately, John sent me an email message suggesting that I should reach out to Jessica Shryack and that I could use his name to warm up the cold call.

I checked out Jessica on LinkedIn and I was confused. I couldn't figure out why John would suggest her. Her profile didn't suggest the specific expertise I was looking for or show the experience as a speaker or facilitator. Here's what Jessica's LinkedIn profile said about her:

Before
Jessica Shryack, Ph.D.

Director of Quality Initiatives at Minneapolis Community and Technical College

I am passionate about people—their concerns, questions, development. I love to see people connect across differences.

Taking a chance, I reached out to Jessica and sent her a LinkedIn invitation with a personal note telling her about my area of interest in civil discourse and that our "mutual friend" John suggested that we connect. She accepted my invitation, and we set up time for a phone call. When we had the chance to meet virtually, I was blown away by her experience, passion, knowledge, and interest in the topic of civil discourse. I was so glad that I called her.

I offered to help Jessica position herself more effectively so that she could attract more speaking and facilitation engagements. I introduced her to the defining paragraph framework and we set up a coaching call over FaceTime. I started our session by asking her to tell me about herself. She said that she usually defines herself by the degree that she has: a Ph.D. She then elaborated on the types of projects and programs that she is often called upon to lead in her job at the college and in the community. The more she spoke, the more interesting she became to me. And to think that all this compelling information was missing from her LinkedIn profile.

At the end of our ninety-minute coaching session, Jessica had created the beginnings of a defining paragraph. It is so much more powerful than her "before" profile. At the time of this writing, here is how Jessica's defining paragraph reads:

After

> My name is Jessica Shryack and I am a leader in higher education, expert facilitator, and keynote speaker.
>
> In my role as the Director of the Quality Initiatives at Minneapolis College, I lead organizational effectiveness efforts through planning, process improvement, and evaluation.
>
> Through my campus work in equity and inclusion and my volunteer leadership, I help people connect across difference using the Living Room Conversations model.
>
> In fact, I have led more than 500 people in both small- and large-group formats to engage in Living Room Conversations on critical topics facing our country, like experiences of race and racism.

As a result of my work, diverse stakeholders are able to come together and have productive conversations and solve complex problems, while enhancing the effectiveness and harmony within their organizations, workplaces, and communities.

On a personal note, I am very interested in mindfulness and spirituality and recently read the research article "Mindfulness Equity and Western Buddhism" by Harrison Blum.

Like all of us, Jessica still has work to do on her defining paragraph. She has decisions to make, changes to consider, external feedback to obtain, and practice to get her comfortable using it in different situations. But she is on her way to positioning herself to attract more of the opportunities and work that she desires. By doing so, Jessica will put herself in position to help more people and create more positive outcomes by sharing her knowledge and skills that she is so passionate about.

Put Yourself Out There

It takes courage and confidence to share your defining paragraph—whether it's in a face to face situation, in a group setting, a job interview, or on your LinkedIn summary. But guess what, you can always change it. You can test it. Get reactions to it. Sit with it and see how you feel about it. Remember that your defining paragraph is first for you, secondly for others. Personal empowerment and self-awareness are just a few of the many benefits you'll get from developing and sharing your defining paragraph.

It is not uncommon for my clients to express some concern about using their new and improved defining paragraphs on LinkedIn or in other situations. They worry that it might sound like they are bragging, or that they are looking for a new job. I understand this feeling and the potential for sending the wrong message. But consider this: if you don't position yourself, who will? People can't read your mind. They don't know what you want or what you are best at. It is up to you to figure that out and to communicate it in a clear, concise, and confident way. As Mark LeBlanc points out in the Preface to Part I of this book, "The way you communicate who you are and what you do will ultimately help you overcome *the greatest single obstacle in the marketplace.*"

Don't let your personal brand languish by waiting months on end to share your defining paragraph on LinkedIn. Upload it today. Practice your defining paragraph out loud to yourself in the mirror or while driving in your car. Role play in various situations with people you trust. Get comfortable with it. Get confident using it. Get new opportunities from it. What are you waiting for?

Focus-Driven Opportunity

Your defining paragraph has many possible applications. I have used it to help create my one-page professional biography, and boiler plate copy at the end of my press releases and articles. I've included it in client proposals. I've adapted the defining paragraph and used parts of it on my website. I have shared it with my referral partners so that they know the kinds of clients and business opportunities that are best suited for me. I have also shared my defining paragraph with colleagues who have offered to facilitate networking introductions for me. The information contained in your defining paragraph is very strategic and useful.

It has also given me a strategic focus and helped control my urge to chase every opportunity that comes my way. Prior to working with the defining paragraph, I had developed more than fifty individual programs. Some of them only sold one time but were still on my menu of goods and services. This not only wasted my time (in development and marketing) but confused my clients and prospects. It was just too much. I was trying to please everyone and in doing so pleased very few. My business and career suffered. So did I. Worse yet, the value that I could bring to the world was diminished from my own lack of clarity and focus.

Since learning about the power of the defining statement, and the power and applications of the defining paragraph, my business has taken off in a very positive direction. I've been much happier with my business results and with myself. Life is good. Business is good. What could be better? Actually, there is something that could make it even better: a powerful story.

Where Are We Headed Next?

In the next part of this book, written by my coauthor and publisher, Henry DeVries, you will discover another tool to add even more fuel, focus, and momentum to your business and career. Get ready to discover your defining story.

PART III
DEFINING STORY

by Henry DeVries

Preface

A tough challenge for many in business is convincing enough prospects to hire them. To become more persuasive, it pays to know how humans are hardwired for stories. If you want prospects to think it over, give them lots of facts and figures. If you want them to decide to hire you, tell them the right story.

Storytelling helps persuade on an emotional level. Maybe that is why so many Fortune 500 companies are hiring storytelling experts to teach their sales and business development professionals to tell relatable stories that will convince prospects.

Consultants, business leaders, speakers, and authors need to know the proper methods of telling a persuasive story. As my buddy Michael Hauge, a screenwriting teacher and consultant to Hollywood filmmakers like Will Smith, says: "The story must be true, but it does not have to be factual." In other words, some literary license is allowed to condense the story down to its essence. It also may be surprising to you when you learn who should be the heroes in the stories you tell to your prospects.

First, you will learn the basics of telling a client success story. Then you can apply those basics to crafting your defining story.

Any story worth telling is worth telling poorly. That is, to start. Practice, practice, practice telling your stories to improve them. Especially the defining story of you. Best wishes on your quest to persuade with your defining story.

Henry DeVries

CHAPTER 7
Craft Your Defining Story

Always remember that humans are hardwired for stories. Many fields of science testify to this truth. Maybe that is why companies like FedEx, Kimberly Clark, and Microsoft are hiring storytelling experts to teach their executives to tell relatable stories. Nothing is as persuasive as storytelling with a purpose, and here you will learn the techniques of telling a great story employed by Hollywood, Madison Avenue and Wall Street.

Three Must-Have Characters

Every story needs a hero (think main character), a nemesis, and a mentor. If you are familiar with *The Wonderful Wizard of Oz*, the main character would be Dorothy Gale of Kansas, the nemesis is the Wicked Witch of the West, and the mentor is Glinda the Good Witch. By the way, if I were to write the plot summary for this book and movie it would be: "Girl arrives in strange land and kills. Makes three friends and kills again." For me it is the ultimate chick flick: two women fighting over a pair of shoes.

If the first *Star Wars* movies are more your cup of tea, then we are talking about Luke Skywalker as the main character, Darth Vader as the nemesis, and Jedi Knight Obi-Wan Kenobi and then Jedi Master Yoda as the mentors. My favorite mentor advice from Yoda is: "Do or do not. There is no try."

Here is more information on the first three steps of the storytelling formula:

Start with a Hero. This is the main character. King Arthur, Sherlock Holmes, and George Bailey in Frank Capra's classic *It's A Wonderful Life* all have something in common. They are the protagonist that propels the story. The first sentence of your story begins with the name of the main character and what he or she wants.

 Next, Introduce the Nemesis. What prevents your main character from getting what he or she wants? Stories are boring without conflict, so the main character needs to be in opposition to another character. Professor Moriarty, nicknamed "The Napoleon of Crime" in the Sherlock Holmes book series, is a master nemesis. So are old man Potter in *It's a Wonderful Life*, the Nazis who want the Lost Ark, and the Wicked Witch of the West in Oz ("I'll get you, my pretty, and your little dog, too!"). Often, the word antagonist is a better term. In business storytelling this is often the government, the competition, or the bad economy.

 Then Add the Mentor. This is where you come in. Heroes can't do it on their own. They need training. Sometimes they need a gentle hand to show them the way or get them back on the right road. Clarence the Angel in *It's a Wonderful Life*, Merlin in the King Arthur Legends, and Gandolf in *Lord of the Rings* are there to fill this critical need.

In my workshops, participants often object to being cast as the mentor instead of the hero. "What we did was heroic—we saved that client," they tell me. "Ah," I tell them, "if you cast yourself as the hero, what role do you give your client?" They answer, "the damsel in distress." Nobody wants to project themselves into the

Stories are boring without conflict.

story as the damsel in distress. Clients want to see themselves as the hero who was smart enough to find the right mentor to overcome the nemesis.

Start your story by introducing us to the main character. Make this person likable. Make us want to root for the main character.

Next, introduce us to the nemesis, or the problem. In one of my stories I label a bad economy as "the wolf at the door." If you can use a person that represents the issue, so much the better.

Finally, you should be the mentor or wise wizard character of the story. With your training or advice your hero/client overcomes the nemesis problem.

Famous Heroes, Villains, and Mentors

 Heroes/Main Characters

King Arthur from King Arthur and Knights of the Round Table Legends

Indiana Jones from *Indiana Jones* and *The Raiders of the Lost Ark*

Scarlett O'Hara from *Gone with the Wind*

Atticus Finch from *To Kill a Mockingbird*

John Galt from *Atlas Shrugged*

Harry Potter from *Harry Potter and the Philosopher's Stone*

Eliza Doolittle from *My Fair Lady*

Rocky Balboa from *Rocky*

Katniss Everdeen from *The Hunger Games*

James Bond from *every single James Bond novel and film ever*

Cinderella from *Cinderella*

Lisbeth Salander from *The Girl with the Dragon Tattoo*

Sherlock Holmes from the Sherlock Holmes stories by Sir Arthur Conan Doyle

Roy Hobbs from *The Natural*

 Villains/Nemesis

Wicked Witch of the West from *The Wonderful Wizard of Oz*

Hannibal Lecter from *Silence of the Lambs*

Norman Bates from *Psycho*

Big Brother from *1984*

Apollo Creed from *Rocky*

Evil stepmother from *Cinderella*

Professor Moriarty from the Sherlock Holmes stories

Judge Banner from *The Natural*

 Mentors

Glinda the Good Witch from *The Wonderful Wizard of Oz*

Jim in *Huckleberry Finn*

Yoda in *Star Wars*

Professor Henry Higgins from *My Fair Lady*

Mickey from *Rocky*

Fairy Godmother from *Cinderella*

Dr. John Watson from the Sherlock Holmes stories

Friar Tuck from *Robin Hood*

Iris from *The Natural*

And Iago from *Othello* (because not all mentors are good mentors)

Eight Great Stories

Next, decide what story you are telling.

There are eight great metastories that humans want to hear over and over again. Almost all works of literature follow these eight basic story structures.

This is based on *The Seven Basic Plots: Why We Tell Stories*, a 2004 book by British journalist Christopher Booker, a Jungian-influenced analysis of stories and their psychological meaning. I compared Booker's eight categories and discovered the same rules apply to the greatest business non-fiction books of all time.

Here are the eight categories:

 Monster. A terrifying, all-powerful, life-threatening monster whom the hero must confront in a fight to the death. An example of this plot is seen in *Beowulf, Jaws, Jack and the Beanstalk*, and *Dracula*. Most business books follow this plot. There is some monster problem in the workplace, and this is how you attack it. Business book examples: *Slay the E-Mail Monster, The E-Myth Revisited, Whale Hunters, Stop Global Boring*, and *Growing Your Business*

 Underdog. Someone who has seemed to the world to be quite commonplace is shown to have been hiding a second, more exceptional self within. Think *The Ugly Duckling, Cinderella, David vs. Goliath, Jane Eyre, Rudy*, and *Superman*. The business books in this category discuss how people raised themselves up from nothing to success—typical rags-to-riches stories. One of my early favorites was *Up From Slavery* by Booker T. Washington (I even got to meet his great-great-grandson and chat about the book). Donald Trump books don't count. He raised himself up from riches to mega riches. Business book examples: *Moneyball, Up the Organization, Grinding it Out*

Comedy. If the main character tries to solve a problem with a wacky idea, that is a comedy. Think of the movies *Tootsie* and *Some Like it Hot*. Following a general chaos of misunderstanding, the characters tie themselves and each other into a knot that seems almost unbearable; however, to universal relief, everyone and everything gets sorted out, bringing about the happy ending. Shakespeare's comedies come to mind, as do Jane Austen's novels like *Sense and Sensibility*. Business book example: *2030: What Really Happens to America, A Whack on the Side of the Head, How I Lost My Virginity, Swim with the Sharks Without Getting Eaten Alive*

 Tragedy. This is about solving a problem by going against the laws of nature, society, or God. Through some flaw or lack of self-understanding, a character is increasingly drawn into a fatal course of action, which inexorably leads to disaster. *King Lear, Othello, The Godfather, Madame Bovary, The Picture of Dorian Gray, Breaking Bad, Scarface*, and *Bonnie and Clyde*—all flagrantly tragic. Business book examples: *Too Big to Fail, Barbarians at the Gate, Liar's Poker, The Big Short*.

 Quest. From the moment the hero learns of the priceless goal, he sets out on a hazardous journey to reach it. Examples are seen in *The Odyssey, The Count of Monte Cristo*, and *Raiders of the Lost Ark*. Business book examples: *The HP Way, In Search of Excellence, How to Win Friends and Influence People, How to Close a Deal Like Warren Buffett, Never Be the Same*

 Escape. The hero or heroine (main character) and a few companions travel out of their familiar surroundings into another world completely cut off from the first. While it is at first wonderful, there is a sense of increasing peril. After a dramatic escape, they return to the familiar world where they began. *Alice in Wonderland* and *The Time Machine* are obvious examples, but *The Wizard of Oz* and *Gone with the Wind* also embody this basic plotline. Business book examples: *The Prodigal Executive, The Innovator's Dilemma, How I Raised Myself from Failure to Success in Selling*

 Rebirth. There is a mounting sense of threat as a dark force approaches the hero until it emerges completely, holding the hero in its deadly grip. Only after a time, when it seems that the dark force has triumphed, does the reversal take place. The hero is redeemed, usually through the life-giving power of love. Many fairy tales take this shape — also, works like *Silas Marner, Beauty and the Beast, A Christmas Carol,* and *It's a Wonderful Life.* Business book examples: *Out of Crisis, Seabiscuit.*

 Mystery. In his book, Booker adds an eighth plot, a newcomer that appeared from the time of Edgar Allan Poe. From the Sherlock Holmes stories to the *CSI* TV series franchise, this basic plot involves solving a riddle, and has gained immense popularity since the mid-1800s. Business book examples: *Good to Great, Think and Grow Rich, The Secret, Atlas Shrugged, Who Moved My Cheese, Cracking the Personality Code.*

The bottom line: Know what story you are telling.

The Simple Six-Step Heroic Storytelling Formula

Any business leader or sales professional can easily use proven techniques of telling a great story—the same ones used by Hollywood, Madison Avenue, and Wall Street—by employing "The Simple Six-Step Heroic Storytelling Formula" to gain the chance to make a proposal or close the sale. (For an in-depth discussion, please see my book *Persuade With a Story!*)

These success stories must be true case studies, but they must be told in a certain way. Here is a quick overview of the formula:

Step One: Start with a main character. Every story starts with a character who wants something. This is your client. Make your main characters likable so the listeners will root for them. To make them likable, describe some of their good qualities or attributes. Generally, three attributes work best: "Marie was smart, tough, and fair" or "Johan was hardworking, caring and passionate." For privacy reasons you do not need to use their real names ("this is a true story, but the names have been changed to protect confidentiality").

Step Two: Have a nemesis character. Stories need conflict to be interesting. What person, institution, or condition stands in the character's way? The villain in the story might be a challenge in the business environment, such as the recession of 2008 or the Affordable Care Act (the government is always a classic nemesis character).

Step Three: Bring in a mentor character. Heroes need help on their journey. They need to work with a wise person. This is where you come in. Be the voice of wisdom and experience. The hero succeeds because of the help you provide.

Step Four: Know what specific kind of story you are telling. Remember, human brains are programmed to relate to one of eight great metastories (monster, underdog, comedy, tragedy, quest, escape, rebirth, and mystery). If the story is about overcoming a huge problem, that is a monster problem story. If the company was like a David that overcame an industry Goliath, that is an underdog story.

Step Five: Have the hero succeed. Typically, the main character needs to succeed, with one exception: tragedy. The tragic story is told as a cautionary tale—great for teaching lessons, but not great for attracting clients. Have the hero go from mess to success (it was a struggle, and they couldn't have done it without you).

Step Six: Give the listeners the moral of the story. Take a cue from Aesop, the man who gave us fables like The Tortoise and the Hare (the moral: slow and steady wins the race). Don't count on the listeners to get the message. The storyteller's final job is to tell them what the story means.

But When Am I the Hero?

Now we have covered the three main characters and the eight great stories. Your turn to be the hero is coming. If you want to attract more clients, then your clients must be the heroes, or main characters, of all your success stories (save one: your defining story—more on that in the following chapter).

CHAPTER 8

When Am I the Hero?
Your Defining Story

There is only one story you get to tell where you are the hero. This is Your Defining Story.

Your presentations, articles, blogs, books, seminars, and speeches should be peppered with such stories. These stories provide the psychological clues as to why prospects should hire you.

Example 1: My Defining Story

Once upon a time, my business coach, Gary Hawk, asked me four questions that changed my life.

First, he wanted to know what the exit strategy was for my San Diego advertising and public relations agency. "Well, Gary, after I run my firm for ten more years, I am turning it over to someone, and then I will teach consultants and coaches how to attract clients," I said. "My wife and I are going to retire to a college town and spend our life surrounded by trees and water."

His second question was, "How would you do that?" I excitedly told him I would write books, make speeches, put on conferences, and teach at a university. There are so many consultants and coaches that are great at what they do, but no one has ever them taught the science of attracting clients.

Gary said, "You sound very passionate," and then asked his third question. "Why are you waiting ten years to follow your passion?" Don't you hate gut-check questions like that? Naturally, that question stumped me because my thoughts were on my obligations, clients, and employees. I described them as "the wolf at my door." In truth, it was my own fear of failure.

The fourth question helped me process: "How could you get started right now in a small way?" "I can send invitations for a free monthly lunch seminar in my office," I ventured. "The sandwiches would be on me and I'd share with consultants and coaches the science of finding clients."

My first free lunch-and-learn seminar was the very next month. The invitations were in the mail when the terrorist attack of September 11, 2001 took place in New York, Washington, DC, and Pennsylvania.

Later that horrible month, much to my surprise, consultants and coaches actually showed up for my lunch seminar. After I explained my theories, the attendees asked how much I'd charge to be their coach. Soon they asked me to write books for them and teach them to give speeches that attract clients. Meanwhile, while five of the top ten advertising and public relations firms in San Diego went out of business, my work helping consultants and coaches to attract clients literally took over my business.

We renamed our company the New Client Marketing Institute. Over the next eight years, I invested $2 million in scientifically researching how to attract high-paying clients. We even tied in with the Harvard Business School. My research revealed a proven way for consultants and coaches to obtain a marketing return-on-investment of 400 percent to 2000 percent. Since then, I've edited or ghostwritten more than 300 business books.

These days, I annually speak to thousands of consultants and coaches, teaching them writing and speaking strategies to attract high-paying clients and how to persuade with a story. In addition to running the New Client Marketing Institute and the Marketing with a Book and Speech Summits, in 2007, I accepted an appointment as assistant dean and a member of the marketing faculty for continuing education at the University of California, San Diego, my alma mater, a campus located in a grove of trees overlooking the Pacific Ocean.

In 2014, my quest took a new turn. I launched Indie Books International. Independent consultants, coaches, and business owners turn to us for help with the preparation, publication, and promotion of a book that grows their business, puts money in the bank, and helps them make the difference they want to make. Indie Books International was founded by two best-selling authors: Mark LeBlanc and myself. We educate consultants and coaches that the publication of the book is the starting line, not the finish line.

I share my story in order to spread a message of encouragement to consultants and coaches who are good at what they do and need to learn the science of attracting high-paying clients.

But this story isn't really about me. It is about you. Here are four questions for you.

1. What is your goal?

2. How would you do it?

3. What are you waiting for?

4. How could you get started in a small way?

Example 2: Larry Haas, author of *SOS To ROI*

The following story is told by Larry Haas:

> While growing up in Colorado in the mid-1980s, I had a dream of going to the Air Force Academy and flying fighter planes, a la *Top Gun*.
>
> Every chance I got, I went on tours of the Academy, drove around the public-access portions of the campus, and learned everything I could about attending one day. I even snagged a precious copy of the cadet handbook and started to memorize the code of conduct. I learned the minute features of historical airplanes so I could recognize them at a glance.

In short, I was a man with a plan.

Naturally, the application process required a comprehensive medical evaluation. I had no worries about this since I played multiple sports, was physically fit, had good eyesight, and did very well in school. I was a shoo-in, right? Yet, when the results came back, the vision section concluded:

'Candidate sees 20/20 but is not qualified for pilot training due to less than plano refractive error in any meridian.'

Really? What's a plano? What's a meridian? *Noooooooooo!*

Now I'm no doctor, and I didn't know exactly what that meant. But what I did know was that for me, the likelihood of becoming a fighter pilot appeared (as far as I could "see") distant. What's worse, now the competition was tougher, because the Academy had most openings dedicated to future pilots. Furthermore, I resided adjacent to Colorado's Fifth Congressional District, which included the Air Force Academy, and was now competing with thousands of other candidates for precious few nonpilot openings and even fewer Congressional nominations. Despite having done well in school and sports, being considered an exceptionally well-rounded guy, and receiving great feedback from my admissions interviews, I didn't make it in.

I was devastated. I was sick.

But I swallowed my pride and did what I thought was the next best thing. I went to school on an ROTC scholarship and studied aerospace engineering. I figured if I couldn't go to the Academy and fly the jets in the sky, at least I could help design and build them on the ground.

When I graduated and entered the Air Force, I was assigned to my dream job: a program manager on the

F-22 fighter jet. At the time, that plane was ending its preliminary design process and was the coolest. It was stealthy, sleek-looking, fast and furious.

As I moved from assignment to assignment, I became adept at quickly grasping the vast array of technologies on this and other airplanes, missiles, satellites, and collections of advanced technologies we can't talk about in this book. And one thing was certain: each came with its challenges, and the companies that build them did some amazing things even though the programs often cost a bit (or a lot) more and took longer than planned.

Through the years since the Air Force, I have come to realize that I enjoy helping companies deal with complex and sophisticated technological and engineering challenges. I'm thankful to have been privy to many mistakes as well as some amazing successes.

Example 3: Craig Lowder, author of *Smooth Selling Forever*

The following story is told by Craig Lowder:

Okay, so here is the truth about me, straight up. I didn't go to Harvard, I didn't go to Stanford, and you won't find a bunch of letters after my name. I once went as far as having MBA on my business card, but you won't find it there anymore.

Mine was a blue-collar family just outside the rust belt, where I learned that it's not only what you know, but how you apply it. I learned a couple of other important lessons back then that still serve me today.

One is that teamwork is a critical component of success anywhere—whether you are playing shortstop on a baseball field, crewing a yacht in the America's Cup, or navigating the challenges of the global economy.

That's why as president of my own sales consulting firm, I only work with clients who are willing to listen, think, and contribute to their own development and their company's success. Success comes to a team, not individuals.

The second is nothing beats experience. I've been mentored by some of the best in the business—people like Brad Sugars, Verne Harnish, Larry Wilson, Jeffrey Gitomer, and Keith Cunningham—but I've really learned the best teacher is experience.

And I've had my share. I have worked with forty-eight B2B and B2C companies, increasing their first-year annual sales from 22 to 142 percent.

But it has not all been smooth selling. Through it all I've seen the good and the bad, and, frankly, learned more from the bad than the good. There have been storms that tested me. It is a real-world perspective that guides my work with growing companies today.

Seven Ways to Persuade with a Story

After you build an inventory of your defining story and client success stories that demonstrate how you take clients from mess to success, you are then ready to deploy the stories. In storytelling, context is everything. You should never randomly tell stories, but instead use stories at the right strategic times.

Here are seven perfect opportunities to persuade with a story:

1. **During an Initial Call to Get a Meeting.** Never lead with your defining story. First have a conversation with

You should never randomly tell stories, but instead use stories at the right strategic times.

the prospect. Ask about their goals, what they are doing right, and what they see as the roadblocks they hope you can help them get past. At this point ask: "May I tell you a true story about how we helped a client get from where you are now to where you want to go?"

2. **To Close a Client During a Meeting.** For many companies, business development is not a one-step close. During an initial get together you gather information and in the subsequent meeting you propose a course of action. This is the time to add a case history story of a client that was in a similar situation.

3. **On a Website.** Get rid of those dry case studies on the website. Instead, convert them to the more persuasive story format of the six-step formula.

4. **In Collateral Material.** Don't just tell when stories will sell. In your brochures and information kits replace drab case histories with persuasive heroic success stories (remember your role is wise mentor).

5. **During a New Business Presentation.** It's fairly common to be asked to make a presentation to a group. Because humans are hardwired for stories, this is a perfect opportunity to make your pitch memorable.

6. **During a Speech, Media Interview or Job Interview.** Occasionally you might get an invitation to make a speech, give an interview to the media, or interview for a job. Illustrate your message with a pithy story. Stories make excellent presentation openers as they have the power to immediately grab the attention of the audience.

7. **To Train Employees on Core Values.** Stories can also be the gift to your business that keeps giving. Reinforce core

values with employees and new hires through sharing the inventory of stories.

To Sum Up: Nothing is as persuasive as storytelling with a purpose. The right stories can work wonders whether you are using them in a one-to-one meeting, in a presentation that is one-to-several, or in a speech or publicity that is one-to-many.

But the Story Doesn't End Here

Start today to build an inventory of persuasive client success stories and your defining story. The final section will help you pull it together and show you how to best take advantage of our defining statement, defining paragraph, and defining story.

PART IV
PULLING IT ALL TOGETHER

CHAPTER 9
Why This Work Matters

Coauthor Kathy McAfee was reminded of the importance of this work after meeting up with her friend and fellow Rotarian, Ron Demonet, at a local coffee house. He wanted to meet with her to discuss the need to develop an elevator pitch for their local Rotary club.

Ron confessed that he sometimes struggles finding the words to communicate his mission. "I want to be good at communicating," he explained. "It's a skill that I am trying to acquire."

As the new club president, Ron was aware of a problem that members were having. He observed how they struggled to explain what we do as Rotarians. He could see the opportunity for all members to serve as ambassadors of the club, but their inability to articulate who we were and what we did as Rotarians was becoming a limiting factor. He wanted to solve this problem by giving them a helpful resource.

The first few drafts were a struggle. Some ideas were floated and then rejected. By the time they left the coffee house, Ron and Kathy had drafted a defining statement for Rotary and a defining paragraph that he would take to the board of directors for feedback. They even brainstormed how they could use the third tool, the defining story.

Ron took immediate action by uploading the defining statement to his LinkedIn profile in the Experience section to describe his job duties as president of the local Rotary club. Ron was pleased to be able to share this new concise communication on his LinkedIn profile.

Kathy suggested to Ron that he take the next step in evolving his LinkedIn profile by crafting his own personal defining paragraph (separate from the one we had developed for Rotary) and sharing it on his LinkedIn profile as his summary statement. Kathy could hear Ron's angst in his audile exhalation. Working on the organization is one thing; working on yourself is a whole lot more difficult. Kathy reminded Ron that it's not enough to do the positioning and branding work for your organization. You, as the leader, have to do it for yourself.

During their meeting Ron shared that he sees communication as a two-fold skill set: 1) Listening and discerning. As Stephen Covey coined it in his book *The Seven Habits of Highly Effective People*, "First seek to understand, before you are understood;" and 2) Being clear and concise in what you say so that people can understand you.

In Kathy's eyes, Ron was a pretty good communicator already, he just needed a little help in figuring out how to express who he is, what he does, and how he can help others. If he can figure that out, he will be able to do more of the work he loves. He will increase the chances of being able to fulfill his personal mission.

This is the goal of this book. To help Ron and people like him to realize their dreams and goals by effectively positioning themselves.

CHAPTER 10

Making It Work for You

You now have a path and a plan to build your business and your career by attracting more prospects, clients, and work engagements that align with your strengths and interests. And it all starts with defining you. And to do this you'll need to have these three tools at the ready:

1. Defining Statement—a single sentence that articulates what you do and for whom

2. Defining Paragraph—seven sentences that highlight your expertise and passions so that others can better connect with you and understand how you can help them or others in their network

3. Defining Story—an authentic and compelling short story about a client success or work experience that demonstrates the value you bring to the table

You might be asking yourself these questions right about now:

Will it be hard work? Yes.
Is it worth it? Definitely.
Can I outsource it? No.
Will I need some help? Most likely.
When do I need to start? Right now.
Will I enjoy the process? Oh yeah!

We wish you great success in your *Defining You* journey. We look forward to hearing how this book helped you succeed.

APPENDIX A

Tools and Rules: A Checklist

This section provides you with a quick reference, so you can more easily put this work into action. You can download pdf-writable versions of these frameworks at https://indiebooksintl.com/learningcenter

Defining Statement—the Framework

The Seven Rules
1. Use eighth grade language.
2. Use conversational language.
3. Use attraction-based language.
4. Use language that is dream-focused versus pain-driven.
5. Use language that contains what you do and who you do it for.
6. Use a dual-focus or two-part defining statement.
7. Use language that can be repeated.

The Four Tips
1. Use one "and" in your defining statement.
2. Keep your outcomes three to five words.
3. Use the words "work with" instead of help, teach, serve, provide.
4. Use the word "want" instead of need.

The Three Tests
1. Will I actually say it in a conversation or introduction?
2. Does it gain attention and attract a prospect?
3. Could another person repeat it or a part of it?

Defining Statement

Who
(markets or types of people you serve)
_____
_____
_____

What
(outcomes and results you produce
for your clients/customers)
_____
_____

**Single Market /
Single Outcome**
_____
_____
_____

**Single Market /
Double Outcomes**
_____
_____
_____

**Single Market /
Triple Outcomes**
_____
_____
_____

**Double Markets /
Single Outcome**
_____
_____
_____

**Double Markets /
Double Outcomes**
_____
_____
_____

**Single Market /
Triple Outcomes**
_____
_____
_____

**Triple Markets /
Single Outcome**
_____
_____
_____

**Triple Markets /
Double Outcomes**
_____
_____
_____

**Triple/Triple
NOT recommended**

X

[Tip] Position yourself for what prospects want (outcomes)
rather than what they need (problems to be solved)

Defining Paragraph—the Framework

The Seven Rules

1. Leverage it strategically.

2. Be introspective.

3. Seek feedback.

4. Forget perfection.

5. Practice out loud.

6. Experiment.

7. Commit it to memory.

The Five Tips

1. Short, simple sentences work best.

2. Stay consistent with your [P] or primary profit center. Tailor your [S] or secondary profit center to fit your audience.

3. Periodically refresh your credibility statement ("In fact...") and your approachability statement ("On a personal note...") to stay current with your experiences.

4. Pause between each sentence.

5. Make eye contact and smile when you share your defining paragraph verbally.

The Three Tests

1. Does it feel natural, authentic, and empowering to share in a conversation?

2. Does it help you and others understand your specific areas of expertise?

3. Does it open the conversation to deeper levels of discussion?

Defining Paragraph

Your Name	Organization's Name
_____	_____

Defining Statement
primary profit center
or area of expertise
[P]
_____
_____
_____

Defining Statement
secondary profit center
or area of expertise
[S]
_____
_____
_____

Credibility
Statement
[C]
_____
_____
_____

Value
Statement
[V]
_____
_____
_____

Approachability
Statement
[A]
_____
_____
_____

[Engage] "Tell me about you and your work."

Defining Story—the Framework

Simple Six-Step Heroic Storytelling Formula

1. Start with a main character.

2. Have a nemesis character.

3. Bring in a mentor character.

4. Know what story you are telling.

5. Have the hero succeed.

6. Give the listeners the moral of the story.

Eight Great Metastories

1. Monster	5. Quest
2. Underdog	6. Escape
3. Comedy	7. Rebirth
4. Tragedy	8. Mystery

Three Main Characters

1. Hero   2. Villain   3. Mentor

One Big Decision: Who should I make the hero of my story: my client? or myself?

Seven Opportunities to Persuade with a Story

1. During an Initial Call to Get a Meeting

2. To Close a Client During a Meeting

3. On a Website

4. In Collateral Material

5. During a New Business Presentation

6. During a Speech, Media Interview, or Job Interview

7. To Train Employees on Core Values

Defining Story

Identify Three Characters

Hero (main character)	*Nemesis* (the problem)	*Mentor* (the helper/guide)

Know what story you are telling (select one of these metastories)

Monster	Underdog	Comedy	Tragedy
Quest	Escape	Rebirth	Mystery

Craft Your Story

1. Introduce the Main Character	2. Identify a Nemesis	3. Bring in a Mentor Character

4. Create Dialogue and Conflict	5. Have the Hero Succeed	6. Moral of the Story

Next Steps: Script it. Practice. Time it. Record it. Get Feedback. Use it. Add it to Your Story Inventory.

APPENDIX B
More Resources

Here is a list of additional resources and professional services to help take your career and business to the next level.

Mark LeBlanc

- Attend one of Mark's Achievers Circle weekend retreats to refocus, recalibrate, and reenergize yourself in order to grow your business.

- Hire Mark as your business development coach. He can help you start a business and grow your business by applying the nine best practices and creating momentum to reach your goals.

- Talk to Mark about licensing opportunities and add a new program or service offering to your coaching or consulting business. The defining statement/paragraph/story framework is available as a full curriculum including a Train-the-Trainer series.

- Book Mark as your keynote speaker for an upcoming conference, convention, or meeting.

- Read Mark's other books: *Build Your Consulting Practice*, *Growing Your Business*, and *Never Be the Same*.

Kathy McAfee

- Hire Kathy to facilitate skills training and professional development classes for you and your team. She specializes in the arts of high-engagement presentations and effective networking. Kathy is also available to coach you one-on-one to help prepare you for an upcoming presentation, or to critique a video performance of a recent presentation that you've given.

- Hire Kathy to coach you in the development of your defining paragraph. Virtual coaching sessions are available via Skype, FaceTime, and Zoom.

- Hire Kathy as your executive coach to help you overcome challenges, leverage your strengths, and prepare you for increased leadership responsibilities.

- Book Kathy as your keynote speaker for an upcoming conference, leadership meeting, Employee Resource Group (ERG) program, professional women's conference, Diversity and Inclusion Summit, or customer conferences.

- Stay motivated and inspired by signing up for Kathy's enewsletter *Elevate: Take Your Talent to the Next Level.* Opt-in at https://www.americasmarketingmotivator. com/#signup

- Read Kathy's other books: *Stop Global Boring* and *Networking Ahead,* 3rd edition.

Henry DeVries

- Partner with Henry and his team at Indie Books International to help you market your business with a book and a speech. No matter at what stage you are, Henry can help you realize your dream of publishing a book (or two or three). Here are some of the professional services that will help you make it happen:

  1. Book Preparation.

     - Schedule a thirty-minute, free phone call with a development editor to help you get clarity on four questions: your goal for creating a book, what assets you have now, what roadblocks are in your way, and how others have made it from where you are to where you want to go.

     - Schedule a ninety-minute creative strategy session

with a development editor on how to position yourself as an expert, grow your business, and increase revenues through marketing with a book.

– Not a writer but still want to publish a book? Hire Henry as your ghostwriter. His six-month custom ghostwriting package includes interviewing you about your expertise and then turning it into a published book with built-in marketing that positions you as an expert and increases revenues through a promotion plan and publicity resources.

– Ready to make it happen? The 120-day plan of attack with a development editor includes: book writing/marketing blueprint session, followed by weekly editor feedback sessions to turn your expertise into more books, more buzz, more blogs, and more business.

2. Book Publishing. Simplify your life while expediting time to market. Work with Indie Books International to get your book out of your head and into print. Complete services include manuscript preparation, book design, production details, book launch.

3. Book Promotion. Leverage your new book to grow your business. Henry can help you promote your book with social media campaigns, online marketing, video support, speaking engagements, and more.

• Hire Henry to coach you in the development of your defining story. Virtual coaching sessions are available on Skype, FaceTime, and Zoom.

• Book Henry as your keynote speaker for an upcoming conference, convention, or summit.

• Sign up for Henry's weekly client-attracting tips newsletter at https://indiebooksintl.com/learningcenter

- Read Henry's other books: *How to Close a Deal Like Warren Buffett*, *Marketing with a Book*, *Persuade with a Story!*, *Self-Marketing Secrets*, and *Build Your Consulting Practice*.

APPENDIX C
Meet the Authors

About Mark LeBlanc

Mark LeBlanc has been on his own virtually his entire adult life. At twenty-two, he was inspired by the two words, "You're fired!" He made a decision to do whatever it would take to make it on his own, in his own business. Over the next ten years, he started, managed and grew a creative, graphics, printing, and mailing business. He sold it in 1992 to speak, coach, and write full time.

Mark is currently based out of Minneapolis. He works with people who want to start a business, and with small business owners who want to grow their business. As a speaker, he conducts keynote presentations from thirty minutes to his nationally-renowned, weekend business development retreat called The Achievers Circle.

LeBlanc has authored or coauthored three other books, including *Growing Your Business, Never Be the Same,* and *Building Your Consulting Practice* with Henry DeVries. His signature book, *Growing Your Business When YOU Are the Business* will be released later this year.

He is a past president of the National Speakers Association (NSA) and the Founder of The Mark LeBlanc Foundation which provides $3,000 grants to entrepreneurs under thirty. The Minnesota Chapter of the NSA created The Mark LeBlanc Award in 1997 and presents this award each year for outstanding service. In 2006, the Minnesota Chapter of the NSA inducted Mark into the state speakers' hall of fame. In 2018 Mark was awarded the Certified Speaking Professional (CSP) designation by the NSA.

On a personal note, Mark will walk the short, 500-mile Camino de Santiago pilgrimage across Spain in 2020, for the fourth time.

He is married to Sweet Ann. They enjoy walking, cooking, watching movies and entertaining friends and family in their home. Mark is a proud uncle. In addition to his own nieces and nephews, he has developed relationships with kids and young adults across the United States who refer to him as Uncle Mark, or Mr. Mark if they are from the South.

Learn more about Mark at his LinkedIn page: https://www.linkedin.com/in/speaker-mark-leblanc-89b311/

About Kathy McAfee

Kathy McAfee is an executive presentation coach and professional speaker and is known as America's Marketing Motivator. Her mission is to help corporate leaders and business professionals to more effectively leverage their talent, energy, and influence to create positive changes in the world.

She is the author of *Stop Global Boring, Networking Ahead,* 3rd edition, and co-author of *Defining You.* She is also the recipient of the prestigious Best Blog of the Year, as awarded by *The Women in Business and The Professions World Awards* (2014).

In her role as executive presentation coach, she helps clients increase their confidence, credibility, and influence by reducing their PowerPoint clutter to better engage their audiences and move them to action. A certified Master Practitioner of Neuro Linguistic Programming (NLP), Kathy shows her clients how to clear their limiting beliefs and use more effective strategies to realize their full leadership potential.

Over a period of thirty years, Kathy has succeeded in numerous corporate leadership positions. She's brought marketing success to organizations like Levi Strauss & Co., Maybelline, Southcorp Wines of Australia and ADVO. On a three-year assignment in England, Kathy led European marketing initiatives for an international vision care company. In 2005, Kathy gave flight to her entrepreneurial dreams and launched Kmc Brand Innovation, LLC, a talent development company offering communication training, executive and business coaching, and keynote speaking services to her motivated clients.

Kathy is a graduate of Stanford University in Economics. She is a member of the National Speakers Association, a past board member for the YWCA of the Hartford Region, and an active member of Rotary International, and Soroptimist International of the Americas. A resilient woman, Kathy is also an ovarian cancer survivor, and holds a second-degree black belt in the martial art of Tae Kwon Do. Kathy and her husband Byron, their rescue dog Sofiya, and three spirited cats are enjoying life in Greenville, South Carolina, USA.

Learn more about Kathy at her LinkedIn page https://www.linkedin.com/in/kathymcafee/ or by visiting her website: https://www.americasmarketingmotivator.com or you can call Kathy at +1 (860) 371-8801.

About Henry DeVries

Henry DeVries is the CEO (chief encouragement officer) of Indie Books International, a company he cofounded with Mark LeBlanc in 2014. He works with independent consultants who want to attract more high-paying clients by marketing with a book and speech.

As a speaker, he trains business development teams and business leaders on how to sell more services by persuading with a story.

He is also the president of the New Client Marketing Institute, a training company he founded in 1999. He is the former president of an Ad Age 500 advertising and PR agency and has served as a marketing faculty member and assistant dean of continuing education at the University of California, San Diego.

In the last ten years, he has helped ghostwrite, edit, and coauthor more than 300 business books, including his McGraw-Hill bestseller, *How to Close a Deal Like Warren Buffett*—now in five languages, including Chinese. He has a weekly column with Forbes.com. He earned his bachelor's degree from UC San Diego, his MBA from San Diego State University, and has completed certificate programs at the Harvard Business School.

As a result of his work, consultants and business owners get the four Bs: more bookings, more blogs, more buzz, and a path and plan to more business.

On a personal note, he is a baseball nut. A former Associated Press sportswriter, he has visited forty-two major league ballparks and has two to go before he "touches 'em all."

His hobby is writing comedy screenplays that he hopes will one day be made into films.

Henry DeVries can be reached at henry@indiebooksintl.com, or call him at 619-540-3031.

Learn more about Henry at his LinkedIn page: https://www.linkedin.com/in/henryjdevries/ or by visiting the website for Indie Books International: http://indiebooksintl.com.

Index

Made in the USA
Columbia, SC
21 December 2018